# A SENTIMENTAL EDUCATION

# A

# SENTIMENTAL

# EDUCATION

## HANNAH
## McGREGOR

WILFRID LAURIER
UNIVERSITY PRESS

*Inspiring Lives.*

Wilfrid Laurier University Press acknowledges the support of the Canada Council for the Arts for our publishing program. We acknowledge the financial support of the Government of Canada through the Canada Book Fund for our publishing activities. The publication of *A Sentimental Education* is supported in part by funding from the Social Sciences and Humanities Research Council. Funding provided by the Government of Ontario and the Ontario Arts Council. This work was supported by the Research Support Fund.

Library and Archives Canada Cataloguing in Publication
Title: A sentimental education / Hannah McGregor.
Names: McGregor, Hannah, author.
Description: Includes bibliographical references and index.
Identifiers: Canadiana (print) 20210388552 | Canadiana (ebook) 20210388587 | ISBN 9781771125574 (softcover) | ISBN 9781771125581 (EPUB) | ISBN 9781771125598 (PDF)
Subjects: LCSH: McGregor, Hannah. | LCSH: Feminism. | LCSH: Feminist theory. | LCSH: Women's studies. | LCSH: Feminists—Canada—Biography. | LCSH: Podcasters—Canada—Biography. | LCGFT: Autobiographies.
Classification: LCC HQ1190 .M34 2022 | DDC 305.4201—dc23--

Cover and interior design by Michel Vrana. Front cover image istock.com.

Every reasonable effort has been made to acquire permission for copyright material used in this text, and to acknowledge all such indebtedness accurately. Any errors and omissions called to the publisher's attention will be corrected in future printings.

Wilfrid Laurier University Press is located on the Haldimand Tract, part of the traditional territories of the Haudenosaunee, Anishinaabe, and Neutral Peoples. This land is part of the Dish with One Spoon Treaty between the Haudenosaunee and Anishnaabe Peoples and symbolizes the agreement to share, to protect our resources, and not to engage in conflict. We are grateful to the Indigenous Peoples who continue to care for and remain interconnected with this land. Through the work we publish in partnership with our authors, we seek to honour our local and larger community relationships, and to engage with the diversity of collective knowledge integral to responsible scholarly and cultural exchange.

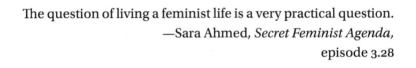

The question of living a feminist life is a very practical question.
—Sara Ahmed, *Secret Feminist Agenda,*
episode 3.28

# TABLE OF CONTENTS

# AUTHOR'S NOTE

I WROTE THIS BOOK BECAUSE I WANTED TO TRY something different. It's an attempt to bring the voice I developed in my work as a podcaster back to my writing, to further push my own understanding of what forms scholarly knowledge might take. That means there are difficult topics in the following pages: some I've tried to grapple with before, like the horrors of white supremacy and settler colonialism, and some that I'm trying to articulate for the first time. I write about my mother's death, disordered eating, and sexual violence. I try to handle these topics with care, knowing that my efforts will be imperfect.

When I first began this book, I thought it was about ideas: white femininity, public intellectualism, embodied knowledges. Then I thought it was about methods: anecdotal theory, feminist friendship. Then I was certain it was about feelings: how we can feel our way through the problems of care and sentiment. It's impossible to fully disentangle these different topics, but I have arrived, at last, at the impossibility of arriving. If this book is about anything, it is about learning as a life-long process, one that navigates ideas, methods, feelings, and texts to continuously move through the complexity of living in a good way.

Being a feminist scholar who works in public and accessible forms, like podcasting, is an ongoing process of trying, fucking up, listening, learning, and trying again. And it's an opportunity not to erase that learning but instead embrace it, understand it as a fundamental part of collective feminist meaning-making and world-building. This book is an extension of my commitment to collective learning as a feminist practice. In part it is a memoir of my own education as a reader and thinker, and in part it is an analysis of the aesthetic modes, genres, and forms that I return to time and again as sites of feminist meaning-making: the sentimental, the personal, the banal, the relatable. It's a meditation on what it means to care deeply—about justice, about revolution, about changing the world—and to know that caring is necessary and yet utterly insufficient. This work will never be perfected, and it will never be completed.

Let's begin.

*—HM*

# TERRITORY ACKNOWLEDGEMENT

I WROTE MOST OF THIS BOOK WHERE I LIVE, ON THE ancestral and unceded territories of the Musqueam, Squamish, and Tsleil-Waututh First Nations. The place currently known as Vancouver is shared between these three Nations. Musqueam territory includes Vancouver as well as parts of what are now called North Vancouver, South Vancouver, Burrard Inlet, New Westminster, Burnaby, and Richmond. Squamish territory includes Gibson's Landing and the Squamish River watershed. Tseil-Waututh territory stretches from the Fraser River to Mamquam Lake, 130 kilometres north of where I am currently sitting.[1] These Nations have inhabited, governed, and stewarded their territories for all of recorded history and beyond; they have always been here, and they will always be here.

But what good is it for me to say so? While acknowledging territory, as an act of protocol, has become increasingly widespread in recent years, critics have pointed out how quickly this gesture becomes rote and emptied of meaning. As Vivek Shraya aptly puts it in her poem "Indian,"

i acknowledge i stole this
but i am keeping it… (2016, l. 12–13)

I began writing *this* section on the back porch of a small cottage on the Amherst Shore in Nova Scotia, which is Mi'kmaq territory. On the flight to this cottage, I read Amy Fung's *Before I Was a Critic I Was a Human Being*, which prompted me to think more seriously about land acknowledgement, not just as a kind of ritualized gesture, but as a personal and political question: what is my relationship to this land? How did I get here, and what am I doing with my presence?

I have never been good with place names: I do not have a geographical sense. I don't know any but the main streets in the cities I've lived in, and I don't know much about the local flora or fauna. What I'm good at remembering are stories, and the way stories attach themselves to the experience of place, how we move through it and make sense of it. I have the same sort of relationship to history, which I tend to remember in terms of patterns and ideas and feelings, not dates or events or people. I used to think this way of engaging with history was a shortcoming.

The personal stories we tell about places are how we locate ourselves within them. The longer our families and people are in a place, the richer and more complex the stories become. My stories, and the stories of my people, are mostly stories of relocation. I read once that settlers fetishize relocation as an ideal because so many of us have lost the connection to our home places. It's a pathology to disdain staying put, a pathology of whiteness. White people have claimed the right to move as often as we[2] wanted, and to force the movement of other peoples and populations—into the cargo holds of ships, into reserves and residential schools, into internment camps, into low-income and ghettoized neighbourhoods, into prisons. Whiteness is also premised on an idea of malleability; as gender studies scholar Kyla Schuller explains in an interview titled "The Trouble with White Women," race has historically been understood in terms of "the differential capacity to be plastic. Whiteness was fully malleable, fully capable of progress or decline, and blackness was…the opposite, barely plastic except for maybe a few years at the beginning of youth" (qtd. in Arjini 2018). This arbitrary nineteenth-century biological categorization has continued to shape the way we talk and think about race, particularly in terms of the treatment of children. Schuller continues: "We can see continuity from [the] 19th-century orphan-train project, which removed Irish-American kids from east-coast cities, to the off-reservation boarding-school movement, which removed tens of thousands of Native American kids from their families, to child detention camps that the Trump administration is running" (2018). To imagine the self as endlessly malleable while claiming the right to violently transform the lives, communities, and lands of others: this is whiteness in action.

My people are all settlers with stories of coming to Canada, stories that are as varied as the places they came from, which is to say a little bit, but not all that much. My maternal grand-father, Edward Penner, was the only one of my grandparents born here, a Mennonite who grew up on a farm just north of Saskatoon, on Treaty 6 land. The Penners came over in the 1890s, part of a major migration of Mennonites out of Russia in search of religious freedom, particularly the right to remain conscientious objectors. Half a century later, there would be another exodus of young Mennonite men away from the farms in Canada to join the military during the Second World War. My grandfather enlisted with the RAF and met my grandmother, Joan, in an Air Force bar in London; she was a year older than him, a Cockney, and eventually a war bride, unprepared, as so many of them were, for the realities of the life she was sailing across the Atlantic to claim. After the war they eventually relocated to Ottawa, which is where my mother was born, and where my brother and I were born. I've never spent time in Saskatchewan, or met that part of my family, and since my mother's death it's been all I can do to maintain a connection with her siblings.

A piece of this story that I never heard, one I've had to put together from reading, is that my Mennonite family's migration was part of the nineteenth-century genocidal project of "settling the West" to drive out and dispossess Indigenous Nations. The Penners were seen as desirable immigrants—less so than the British or Americans, certainly, but still high in the hierarchy of whiteness, valued for their farming skills and ability to produce more white children for a white empire. I doubt my Mennonite family had much concept of their complicity in an ongoing genocide, but the thing about complicity is that it doesn't need to be deliberate to be real. I imagine they were perfectly happy to be swept up in the promises of whiteness and empire and *terra nullius*.

With their Mennonite father who had cut ties with his home, and their English mother who had done the same, my mother and her siblings didn't feel particularly rooted in Ottawa. They all married folks who had come from away—Calabria, Guyana, Scotland—and mostly left as well, moving to Burnaby and Fort McMurray and Sault Ste. Marie, places where there were jobs to be had and property to be bought for cheap. My father was born in Scotland to solidly middle-class Scots who relocated their young children to Canada in the fifties. During a year abroad at the University of Edinburgh, I learned that my grandparents' sense of Canada as a good place to live was no coincidence. They came from a Highland clan, a people whose own relationship to land was violently disrupted by the British empire, which disintegrated the clan system, turned the Highlands into farms for English landowners with enclosure, and relocated Highlanders to a new colony across the ocean, where they were put to work dispossessing other nations and attempting to disintegrate their way of life in turn. My brother and I were born in Ottawa, but again without much sense of it being our place. We were Scottish and English and Mennonite, and encouraged to think of ourselves in those ways. I can't remember a time in my life when I assumed I would stay in Ottawa: leaving felt inevitable.

It wasn't until 2014, living in Edmonton and working on a postdoc at the University of Alberta, that I started to learn about territorial acknowledgements, what the protocol meant, and how to think about being in good relation to a place. I joined a reading group of settler scholars who wanted to learn more about the colonial structures of the university and how we might contribute to decolonizing them. We read the work of Eve Tuck and K. Wayne Yang, whose article, "Decolonization is Not a Metaphor" grounded our thinking in the need to take tangible action; we read and tried to understand Treaty 6 and the obligations that came from it. That's when I started learning how to find out the stories of the places I lived. I came to see my rootlessness as a kind of settler sickness, both a product and cause of the forced relocation of peoples in the service of empire. This learning has continued in Vancouver, where I am witness to settlers, immigrants, and Indigenous visitors from other nations who are trying to learn what it means to be a guest on the territory of the Musqueam, Squamish, and Tsleil-Waututh Nations. I return often to a poem in Jessica Johns' chapbook *How Not to Spill* called "Will the Water Hear Me if I Call Them in Cree." Johns, a member of Sucker Creek First Nation in Treaty 8 territory in Northern Alberta, reflects on her relationship with the ocean, asking,

What does it mean for your body to be here? .... Can you even love right on stolen land? How do you flirt with a water that doesn't want you? (2018, 37)

This is a relationship to place much richer and more complex than being an insider or outsider, one invested in the question of what it means to be in good relation when you, like the blackberries you pick in summer, are "invasive" (35). Johns concludes the poem asking how living here, living with the ocean, might impact future ancestors:

Will they remember how to be here? Will they leave their
hair with yours? Will they spill rocks for you too? (2018, 37)

I'm still learning how to trace my own histories and listen
to my own ancestors, a wisdom I am learning from Indigenous
and Black thinkers. Whiteness, after all, is constructed without
origin or identity; it is unmarked and unmoored deliberately,
so it can function as a hegemonic totality, always reshaping
itself to the present. I wonder if looking to my own roots might
be a way to resist the totalizing power of whiteness. I wonder
if my ancestors, in all their deep imperfections, can teach me
another way.

In 1905, my great-great-grandfather helped to establish the
one-room Penner schoolhouse in what is now called Clark's
Crossing. Only decades earlier, in 1871, the Crown had signed
Treaty 6 with the Plains and Woods Cree and Assiniboine
Nations. One of the terms of Treaty 6 was on-reserve education.
Shortly after the treaty was signed, the Government of Canada
introduced the residential school system, with the first school
opening in 1883. The residential school system was designed to
remove Indigenous children from their homes and communities, a fundamental violation of the treaties the government
had signed. The last school, St. Michael's Indian Residential
School in Duck Lake, was closed in 1996.[3] Its location was less
than 100 kilometres north of the Penner schoolhouse. This is a
history I have been learning, perforce, from a distance. I have
never been to Clark's Crossing or the Penner schoolhouse.

Ottawa is the territory of the Algonquin Nation, but I
didn't know this until very recently, when I saw Métis scholar

Zoe Todd tweet about her own work to be a good guest on Algonquin land. The Algonquins were active in the fur trade, fighting (and losing) alongside the French in the Seven Years' War. The wars fought by colonial powers over the possession of Canada bred new wars between Indigenous Nations, fuelled by firearms and capitalism. There is perhaps no clearer symbol of the Algonquin people's dispossession by the settler government than Algonquin Park. Established in 1893, it is the oldest provincial park in Canada, and one of the most popular, 7,630 square kilometres of land stolen from the Algonquins, named after them, and used for recreation by settlers. The landscape of Algonquin Park has become visual shorthand for Canada through the work of the Group of Seven and Tom Thomson, whose state- and industry-funded landscape paintings helped reinvent Indigenous lands as tourist destinations, portrayed as wild and untouched rather than inhabited and stewarded for tens of thousands of years. As a child I enjoyed visiting the National Gallery, and I loved seeing Tom Thomson's work most of all, because of the way it transformed sights I was familiar with from family vacations into Art. I learned that Thomson had mysteriously disappeared from Canoe Lake in Algonquin Park in 1917. I read Margaret Atwood's *Surfacing* and learned to think of the land around me as a place where white people went to have tragic or mystical experiences. I didn't know the history of this place, I only knew the stories that had been told to erase that history.

---

The place where I was sitting when I first wrote this is Mi'kmaq land as well as the area where Black Loyalists were relocated after the American Revolution. I also learned, from Fung's book, about the relocation of many Beothuk to this land, a correction to what I'd been taught of Beothuk extinction. The story of Indigenous disappearance is precious to white settler Canadians; it lets us feel sad about a genocide that we can locate firmly in the past while denying that we continue to perpetuate it in the present. *If you're already gone,* we seem to think, *it's fine that we've taken your land and aren't planning to give it back.* The introduction to *Songs of the Great Dominion,* the first anthology of Canadian poetry published in 1889, refers to "vanishing races singing their death-song as they are swept on to the cataract of oblivion" (Lighthall 1889, xxi), while in 1920, Duncan Campbell Scott, a canonized poet and Head of the Department of Indian Affairs, declared his plan to "continue until there is not a single Indian in Canada that has not been absorbed into the body politic" (qtd. in McDougall 2008). It's breathtaking how much killing has had to happen to actualize the myth of Indigenous disappearance.

I live in Vancouver now, which is the unceded territory of the Musqueam, Squamish, and Tsleil-Waututh First Nations. I have called myself an uninvited guest here, but that's just a polite term for a home invader. I own a condo here now, and until the COVID-19 pandemic narrowed my world down to how far I can walk in an hour, I worked just blocks from the Downtown East Side, an epicentre of the Missing and Murdered Indigenous Women and Girls crisis, as well as the drug poisoning crisis that has, at least up to the Omicron variant's appearance, killed more people in Vancouver than the virus.

Because I moved to Vancouver more recently, I have learned about this city in a different way. I've learned about it as an adult, for one. I've also learned about it as a teacher, scholar, and feminist. In recent months I've learned about it as a person living through a pandemic, less mobile than ever before and thus more attuned to the city's rhythms and seasonal changes. And I've learned about it from stories. I've heard the stories that poets and writers tell at the readings I've attended; I've heard the stories Musqueam and Squamish Elders share when they introduce events; I've heard the stories my students tell of what their lives are like in this city. I've heard stories about what the land was like before settlers came, about how Chinese workers were treated by white settlers in the nineteenth century, about the Internment of Japanese Canadians in the Second World War, and the Komagata Maru incident.

I've read stories about Vancouver as well: Larissa Lai's *The Tiger Flu* (2018), Eden Robinson's *Trickster Drift* (2018), and Alex Leslie's *We All Need to Eat* (2018). In fact, when I first arrived, a lot of the place names registered to me as references to books, like George Bowering's *Kerrisdale Elegies* (1984) and Daphne Marlatt's *Steveston* (1974). And all of these stories—the ones I've read, heard, overheard, and been told directly—are overlaid onto the space of the city as I navigate it through the banal routes and routines of my daily life. I'm good at remembering stories, which is why I became a literary scholar. Stories are my work now. But stories don't interpret themselves; they unfold in relation to the reader, just as a city is not an objective place, but a site of interdependence and cohabitation. As

I learn, again and again, what it means to live the impossible contradiction of being a white woman and a settler on unceded lands, I must begin with the question of where I am standing, now, and how I got here.

# A
# SENTIMENTAL
# EDUCATION

**FOR AS LONG AS I HAVE BEEN AWARE OF MYSELF AS A WHITE** woman—in the political and theoretical ways one becomes aware of having an identity—I've looked to texts to help me grapple with this problem. I was drawn to books in which other white women tried to model the possibilities of an ethics of care that builds connection across boundaries of difference, books like Camilla Gibb's *Sweetness in the Belly* (2006) and Kim Echlin's *The Disappeared* (2010). In the broader field of normative ethics, an ethics of care is a feminist intervention that grapples with the problem of the other and how we ought to treat them. There are different approaches to producing a normative ethics—an idea of how we ought to be toward one another—such as utilitarianism, which holds that we should make choices that benefit the greatest number of people. The feminist force of an ethics of care lies in how it values the kinds of emotional labour and care work that builds and sustains networks, and that are often responsible for keeping the most vulnerable—those who might be tossed aside in a utilitarian model—alive. Care then leads us toward recognizing complicity: how, via global structures like white supremacy, imperialism, and late-stage capitalism, we are entangled in the lives and well-being of people who live across the world from us.

But compassion, empathy, and care are also burdened with the legacy of white supremacy. The care of white women, I have learned, can be a dangerous thing. One of the foundational texts that taught me this—and showed me new ways to think about what it means to be a white settler in a white supremacist and settler colonial place—is Christina Sharpe's *In the Wake: On Blackness and Being* (2016). In it, Sharpe recounts the history of the slave ship *Zong* which, in 1781, was transporting abducted Africans from West Africa to the Caribbean. After some navigational errors caused them to overshoot Jamaica, the captain "decided to jettison some of the enslaved," causing the owners to sue the underwriters for the insurance on their lost human cargo (Sharpe 2016, 35). What brought me up short when I first read this account is the fact that the *Zong* had originally been named the *Zorg*, the Dutch word for "care." Sharpe says this fact should give pause, so pause I did. A feminist ethics of care invested in witnessing and empathy felt like a starting point for imagining how we might be in relation to one another without causing harm. But I needed to recognize and understand a past and present in which care has, again and again, harmed people.

As I peel back the layers of this problem, I keep returning to texts and, at a sort of meta level, the question of what texts (and reading) are for. If I want to claim that texts are how I learn about myself and my place in the world, then I need to believe that engaging with culture—books, films, and podcasts—can open up possibilities to act, think, and feel otherwise. The problem of being a white woman is also a problem of searching for stories that can teach me how to be in the world as *this* white woman.

Time and again, for me as for many cultural critics, this problem has circulated around the fraught nature of sentimentality, the stories that make space for feeling, for care, for the movement of affect across geographical and cultural borders. My concern with sentimentality in general and sentimental culture in particular has much less to do with aesthetic questions about whether this is "good" art (a hierarchy of culture seems useless to me) than it does with how the culture we love teaches us how to be in, and think about, the world. For me, that education in thinking and feeling through stories has been a sentimental education.

---

I was raised on sentimentality: girl heroines whose pluck and imagination and capacity for care elevated them above other girls—in a world where girlhood itself had no innate value— and instead made them remarkable, noteworthy. I was raised on *Pride and Prejudice*'s Elizabeth Bennett and *Anne of Green Gables*'s Anne Shirley and *Little Women*'s Jo March, on *The Little Mermaid*'s Ariel and *Beauty and the Beast*'s Belle, all queer girls just a little out of step with the world around them, prone, as I was, to bookishness and flights of imagination and perhaps to an unbecoming surplus of feeling that somehow convinced them, despite the restraints of their worlds, not to settle, not to comply, to "want much more than this provincial life."[1] And they were rewarded, these plucky girls—who were all, it would take me years to realize, white—by beauty and marriage and some level of material comfort.

I recognized myself, a precociously smart white girl, in these heroines, and also knew that their story would not be my story until I solved the central problem of me, which was my fatness. Being fat can be radicalizing, if you let it, but sometimes it takes a while. I had a youthful conviction that I, too, had the stuff of a sentimental heroine buried beneath the body I'd been taught to think of as "not me," but a thing I must be liberated from. This conviction was amplified by the domestic tragedy I lived through for most of my youth. My mother was diagnosed with cancer when I was eight and died by suicide at the age of forty-four, when I was sixteen. As much as I was shaped by my mother, by the person she was, I was also shaped by the fact of her death and the stories I told myself to try to make sense of it.

I begin here, with my body and with my mother, because these are the objective facts about me. I'm beginning with the objective: what I have observed, recorded, experienced. This is how Manulani Aluli-Meyer, a scholar of Indigenous Hawaiian epistemologies, explains objectivity, as something located in the body: "Body is a synonym for external, objective, literal, sensual, empirical" (2006, 266). The objective is what we can count: I had one mother, and then I had none. We were four, and then we were three. What comes next, the subjective, the mind, is how we make sense of what we have observed; this is what I call theory, and what Aluli-Meyer calls "logic, rationality, intelligence, conceptualization" (272). We err when we mistake subjectivity for objectivity, when we begin with the interpretation and pretend that it isn't an interpretation at all but a statement of fact, when we begin with the theory and discard any experiences (especially those of marginalized peoples) that don't fit. But theories are damned seductive, and they can make the raw stuff of experience hurt a whole lot less.

The first theory I learned was the stories that taught me how to reframe my mother's sickness and death as sentimental. One of my favourite songs as a child was "I Dreamed a Dream," Fantine's heart-rending ballad from the musical *Les Misérables*. *Les Mis*, as it's referred to by fans, was the first musical my mother took me to; we owned the original cast recording on cassette, and on long summer afternoons we'd pitch a tent in the backyard and listen to it on our portable cassette player. In the musical (an adaptation of a Victor Hugo novel that I have absolutely never read), Fantine is a young woman with an illegitimate daughter she supports by working in a factory. When the lascivious foreman discovers that she is sending her wages to an innkeeper and his wife who are raising her daughter, Cosette, she is fired and, after selling her hair and teeth, eventually turns to sex work. In my childish memory it is unclear that anything more specific than generalized tragedy leads to her death. I would play "I Dreamed a Dream" on the piano, singing along and crying as I imagined my mother speaking the words:

I had a dream my life would be
so different from this hell I'm living.... (Kretzmer 1987)

The hell was her body that wouldn't stop growing tumours, no matter how much she might have wanted to live. An even more sure-fire guarantee of my tears was Fantine's deathbed song, "Come to Me," in which the hero Jean Valjean promises to take care of Cosette after Fantine's death. Her dying words, ending on a frail ascending fifth, are "tell Cosette I love her and I'll see her when I wake." I love that ascending fifth, especially when it's delivered, as some Fantines do, a little flat. The sweet poignancy of Fantine's final delusion marks Cosette forever as a child who was loved, a mark that also makes her special, a heroine.

Helpfully for me, sentimental heroines almost always had dead mothers. Their stories gave me a script, a kind of narrative theory: in addition to suggesting I could ask more of life, they also made sense of a loss I could not otherwise grasp. Sentimental narratives became a replacement for actually feeling what was happening. They told me what to do; they gave me a repertoire of gestures to express a pain that I had no language for. They gave my feelings a vocabulary and, perhaps most importantly at the time, imbued my sorrow with a daintiness, rooted in white femininity, that my own fatness and unhinged grief disallowed.

———

Those sentimental narratives that gave me so much comfort as a child, that provided a kind of theoretical framing for my grief, have a long history dating back to the eighteenth century, when writers and philosophers began pushing back against the Enlightenment's intense investment in rationality. Sentimentality is an appealing way of approaching texts and our relationship to them, offering, as it does, an understanding that is rooted in feeling and care, rather than in patriarchal ideals like rationality and realism. It is also an overdetermined way of relating to the world, mediating identity and experience to give them pleasing shapes and, more significantly, serving a politics invested in smoothing over difference via feeling. While not synonymous with middlebrow, sentimental texts often circulate as middlebrow, a form of culture that is broadly appealing but still somehow "improving," like book club-friendly novels or prestige television dramas. Middlebrow works are also highly mediated; they rely on the legitimizing force of institutions like literary festivals or prizes, best-of lists, or public reading events (Canada Reads being perhaps the best-known Canadian example). Alongside mediation, scholar Beth Driscoll identifies a number of other defining characteristics of the middlebrow: it is also middle-class, reverential, commercial, feminized, emotional, recreational, and earnest (2014, 17–43). Sentimentality, alternatively, is generally (though not always) a characteristic of the culture itself; sentimentality is about heightened attention to feeling, verging sometimes on mawkishness or self-indulgence, and occupies the terrain of feminized, emotional, and earnest culture that Driscoll describes. While the middlebrow is a form of mediation that we can observe in the inner workings of various cultural industries, sentimentality is an aesthetic and generic quality—which raises the question of whether it is innately present in certain texts, or read *into* those texts. We can and do read sentimentally. A favourite childhood book, for example, may be read through the lens of your emotional attachment to it. But we can also read sentimental narratives unsentimentally—as critics do when they read against the grain of sentimental novels—to better understand their cultural work. What sentimental readings and sentimental texts have in common is the framing of sentimentality itself as feminized and emotional.

Sentimentality has historically been disparaged in such a self-evidently misogynist way that attempts at feminist recovery were inevitable, and it continues to be disdained and celebrated by turns. Scholars Kelly McWilliam and Sharon Bickle, for example, point to how sentimental texts have functioned historically to create empathy that, in turn, moulded cultural values; the sentimental, for them, is particularly useful in the context of education, since it's so good at making people care about things they may not have cared about before (2017, 84). Kyla Schuller agrees that sentimentality has a pedagogical function but disagrees that it's teaching anything good. Instead, she reads it as a technology of whiteness that, in the nineteenth century, helped to produce an understanding of white people as the sole representatives of civilization because of a heightened capacity for sympathetic feeling (2018, 2). In *The Biopolitics of Feeling*, Schuller unpacks the role sentimentality played in the invention of race and sex—a history that's worth spending a little more time with.

Schuller's work explores the concept of impressibility which, in keeping with nineteenth-century theories of biological race, was understood as a characteristic associated with whiteness: it essentially meant that white people were malleable, capable of evolving, and thus uniquely capable of civility (2018, 7). But to be impressible was to be permeable, vulnerable to collective feelings and experiences, qualities also ascribed to racialized children to justify violent abduction from their families, and systematic attempts, on the part of imperial powers and colonial governments, to destroy their cultures. Once impressibility was determined to be the quality that distinguished white people as inherently civilized—and racialized children as potentially civilizable—the problem became how to manage *excess* impressibility. What to do with this flow of feeling that both marked white people as more evolved, and put them at risk from ostensibly dangerous outside influences?

Schuller points to two concepts that emerged in the nineteenth century to help manage the dangers of excessive impressibility: sex difference and sentimentalism. As she explains, while the concept of race facilitates the *development* of civilization, "sex difference stabilizes civilization" (2018, 16). Sex divided the civilized population into "the sentimental woman, who possessed both a heightened faculty of feeling and a more transparent animal nature, and the less susceptible and more rational man, thereby relieved from the burdens of embodiment" (16). Sentimentality, then, was an expression of white people's heightened capacity for *appropriate expressions* of feeling, and a set of techniques to manage the potential overflow of feeling, by assigning it to half of the population, as well as regulating its proper expression. Sentimentalism became one of many ways that white women's potential *overabundance* of emotion—the too-much-ness of our empathy and openness to the world—could be disciplined. Other techniques included emerging discourses of "good taste," the redesign of domestic interiors, temperance movements, and the rise of diet culture and cookbooks (18-19). This gendered policing of women's bodies was, and is, part of white supremacy's constitution of white women as responsible for civilization's emotional side, and thus always vulnerable to sensory excess.

The debates about whether the sentimental ought to be recovered or rejected continue to play out in contemporary examples. Melissa Smyth, in a critique of the viral online photography project *Humans of New York*, describes sentimentality as offering "an escape from the difficult conclusions that must come from honest scrutiny of social reality," and argues that sentiment turns emotion into its own endpoint rather than spurring social action (2015). The purpose of reading a *Humans of New York* post, or even donating to one of its charitable initiatives, is to individualize structural problems such that we can imagine solving them simply by feeling strongly enough. But for Leslie Jamison, author of *The Empathy Exams*, the intensity of feeling evoked by sentimental texts isn't a problem (2014). Just because "art makes us feel deeply," she insists, doesn't mean that it only makes us feel: "there can be a sort of second stage to that feeling where we reflect on why those feelings happen and how they might guide us going forth" (qtd. in Narula 2014).

For these writers, as for me, the question of sentimentality's political value is tied up with the question of how or whether feelings lead us to action. When I cry watching a movie or reading a book, does that emotional response spur self-reflection? Or does it begin and end with the cathartic release of tears? Does it trigger an empathetic identification with distant others that meaningfully shifts my political actions? Or does it secure my attachment to whiteness by dehumanizing others? Unsurprisingly, there's a similar debate within middlebrow studies asking whether middlebrow culture can also have an emancipatory impact, perhaps by creating larger publics around significant books that can, in turn, spur necessary cultural conversations. Sentimentality and these debates around middlebrow culture raise similar questions: what do we expect cultural production to do? What is the proper way to engage with culture? How do we know if a work of art has been successful? How much of the onus of transformation lies in the work of art, and how much in the audience?

The belief that reading the right kinds of texts in the right kinds of ways can make us better is hardwired into the origins of the sentimental novel.[2] This origin is generally tied to the work of Jean-Jacques Rousseau, whose 1761 novel *Julie, or the New Heloise*—a philosophical treatise on the importance of authentic feeling in lieu of rational moral codes—was, according to book historian Robert Darnton, the biggest bestseller of the eighteenth century (1984, 242). When I teach the history of publishing and social change, I always pause over the role of the sentimental novel, which has been linked to protests against child labour and vivisection, hospital and prison reform, and most notably the abolition of slavery. Sentimentality is often used to render the suffering of the other legible and sympathetic, making it a good fit for art seeking—to paraphrase Dolly Parton's Christmas special, *Christmas on the Square*—to change minds by first changing hearts. It's tempting to let these histories tell a story about the capacity of literature to promote social change, especially when the books are bestsellers, the evidence of readership and social impact ample, and the historical timeline equally suggestive.

Perhaps the most iconic example, in the United States at least, is Harriet Beecher Stowe's 1852 novel *Uncle Tom's Cabin*, which has been directly linked by many literary historians to the abolition of slavery in the United States. A popular but likely apocryphal story describes Abraham Lincoln meeting Stowe for the first time and asking her, "Is this the little woman who made this great war?" Apocryphal or not, this image of a tiny woman changing the world through the emotional impact of her writing remains popular with people who want, very badly, to believe in the transformative power of literature—and to attach the abolition of slavery to the good deeds of benevolent white ladies rather than the radical organizing and resistance of African Americans.[3] And certainly Stowe was writing with abolition on her mind. As literary scholar Barbara Hochman explains, it was Stowe's goal to establish "sympathetic identification as a widespread reading practice for consuming the story of slavery" by "break[ing] through what she saw as the defences of readers who could hear about slavery every day and never 'listen'" (2004, 143–44). By using sentimental motifs to frame the problem of slavery, Stowe drew on the pleasures of familiar generic conventions to appeal to her white middle-class readership, particularly by making African American characters legible as human beings according to the terms of sentimentality—that is, to depict them feeling deeply. Rousseau's idea of natural and authentic human feeling as the guiding force for moral decision-making is repurposed in Stowe's novel as a means of extending this conception of humanity to include enslaved people. And, while it is often difficult for literary historians to make a solid claim about the social impact of literature, *Uncle Tom's Cabin* was such a phenomenal bestseller that its impact is much easier to establish; it is frequently cited as the bestselling book of the nineteenth century, after the Bible.

Historically, sentimental narratives have been imagined as juxtapolitical, to borrow Lauren Berlant's phrase; they rubbed up against the masculinized political public sphere, but they weren't part of it, because women weren't part of it. That's because popular understandings of the public sphere in the eighteenth and nineteenth centuries, leading up to the suffrage movements of the early twentieth century, explicitly excluded women, who were thought to belong more properly to the domestic sphere, which in turn was affiliated with morality and emotion. This construction of women as the moral drivers of the nation, despite their exclusion from public life, was deeply raced and classed as, indeed, was the suffrage movement. The gendered sphere of sentimentality is the realm of power for middle-class and non-disabled white women; these were the women responsible for the moral virtue of the nation, as well as its literal reproduction. Nineteenth-century Americanist scholar Sarah Mesle reminds us that stories of white women's domestic constriction were *stories* that actively worked "to conceal the ways in which white women were hardly passive 'angels in the house'—they aggressively perpetuated the unfreedom of people and women of color" (2021). Fantasies of white women's constriction are built on the concealed architecture of white supremacist violence.

We can see the construction of white women as domestic angels and moral guides in other classic sentimental novels like Samuel Richardson's *Pamela; or, Virtue Rewarded*, which links together a moral code, depth of feeling, and femininity. Not all sentimental novels are as overtly political as *Uncle Tom's Cabin*, but they are generally as concerned with the question of what is right. This is usually where I caution my students against being too quick to embrace the potential of sentimental narratives to create social change. If sentimentality has been the purview of white women, it has also been activated by images of people of colour suffering.[4] The sentimental heroine is moved to tears by what she sees, as is the reader by what she reads. The heroine and the reader are purified by their feeling, and their feeling in turn establishes their moral superiority as part and parcel of white femininity. At the heart of sentimental narratives is a familiar claim: that the world changes when white women feel sad about it.

We can tell how fundamentally conservative this kind of social change is, by noticing how rooted it remains in fantasies of white purity. James Baldwin argues as much in his essay "Everybody's Protest Novel," in which he quickly establishes his disdain for sentimental novels, describing *Uncle Tom's Cabin* as "a very bad novel, having, in its self-righteous, virtuous sentimentality, much in common with *Little Women*" (1984, 14). His critique of sentimentality, however, is not simply aesthetic, but grounded in his understanding of its political failings, concerned as it is less with social transformation than with the moral panic of white authors and readers, a moral panic that, in the case of *Uncle Tom's Cabin*, expresses itself as a desire to abolish slavery in order to re-establish the moral purity of white women. Protest novels like this are, for Baldwin, comforting rather than disruptive: "Whatever unsettling questions are raised are evanescent, titillating; remote, for this has nothing to do with us, it is safely ensconced in the social arena, where, indeed, it has nothing to do with anyone, so that finally we receive a very definite thrill of virtue from the fact that we are reading such a book at all" (1984, 19). If the thrill of virtue that came from reading *Uncle Tom's Cabin* translated itself into the thrill of virtue caused by white Americans adopting racial liberalism, that suggests less that the novel propelled social change and more that such texts reflect our feelings back to us in a more flattering light. Racial liberalism, after all, was much more interested in tackling white people's feelings about racism than meaningfully addressing the impact of systemic racism on people of colour.[5] Historical examples like *Uncle Tom's Cabin* invite us to ask serious questions about the relationship between literature and the transformation of the social and political status quo. It's a question those of us invested in the transformative possibilities of literature and culture in general come back to again and again: what can reading actually *do*?

This question of the value of reading is a historical and contemporary one. Most recently it came to a head around the circulation of anti-racist reading lists alongside the 2020 Black Lives Matter protests against police brutality. In "What Is an Anti-Racist Reading List For?" Lauren Michele Jackson wonders what these lists actually accomplish: "The syllabus, as these lists are sometimes called, seldom instructs or guides. It is no pedagogue" (2020). Implicit in the creation of these lists is a belief that reading alone—or perhaps even just the stated desire to read, the conspicuous acquisition of books—is sufficient to transform one's view of the world. As an extension of that logic, these lists position works of literature as anti-racist primers, inviting readers to engage with them extractively or, as Jackson puts it, *zoologically*. Works like Octavia Butler's *Kindred* (1979) or Colson Whitehead's *The Underground Railroad* (2016) are stripped of their literary complexity, their concerns with language and narrative structure, and reframed as almost anthropological views into the lives and histories of Black people. Because the purpose of these lists is to foster the self-improvement of the implicitly or explicitly white reader, what is in the books themselves is much less important than how they signify on a shelf or in an Instagram post.

But here's the thing: any generalized belief that reading makes people better, or less racist, or more compassionate, falls apart as soon as we look at the political actions of highly literate cultures. There's just no evidence to support this idea. And yet, for those of us who have built our identities, communities, even our careers around books and reading, there endures a commitment to the experience of how books have changed us. Perhaps these results are not reproducible, but we seem determined to believe that they could be, if we just got the reading list right, or the accompanying syllabus, or the list of discussion questions. Surely what we read shapes us to some extent—but how?

---

As a young reader of sentimental stories, I had no sense of the literary history I have just sketched. But it shouldn't be surprising that a child embedded equally in white femininity and domestic tragedy was drawn to narratives in which intensity of feeling is a sign of virtue. Looking back over my own education as a reader, I was prompted to return to my bookshelves and compile a different sort of reading list: the books that shaped me, books with sentimental value, that I inherited or received as gifts from my mother or grandmother.[6] The list included Margaret Wise Brown's *The Runaway Bunny*, Dennis Lee's *Lizzy's Lion*, Louisa May Alcott's *An Old-Fashioned Girl* and *Little Women*, and Jane Austen's *Pride and Prejudice*. Let me pause for a while over this list. If this were the reading list for a course, what course would it be? What kind of education did these books provide me? What did I make of them then, and what do I make of them now?

*The Runaway Bunny* is an illustrated children's book written by Margaret Wise Brown and illustrated by Clement Hurd, the duo behind *Goodnight Moon*. Originally published in 1942, it has remained a classic of children's literature. It tells the story of a little bunny who wants to run away from his mother, and who imagines the various transformations that might allow him to do so: he tells her he will become a fish in a stream, a rock on the mountain, and a crocus in a hidden garden. His mother replies by imagining her own transformation into a figure who could recapture him in his new form: a fisherman, a mountain climber, a gardener. If he is a bird, she will be a tree; if he is a sailboat, she will be the wind. Their dialogue, illustrated with small black-and-white sketches, is interspersed by full-colour double-page spreads in which their transformations are visually realized: the bunny has become a flower, and his mother is dressed in overalls and a red hat, carrying a hoe over her shoulder. When I was a child, this book was a story about the stability of maternal love as well as my own malleability (or impressibility, Schuller might say). It promised that, no matter how I pushed boundaries and changed myself, my mother's love would follow me, that it was not only unconditional but endlessly adaptive. Little did I know, as a child reader, that Brown was, in the words of journalist Susannah Cahalan, "a 'bisexual rebel' who didn't like kids" (2017). In fact, Brown was one among many queer mid-century children's authors, joining the ranks of Arnold Lobel, James Marshall, Edward Gorey, Tomie dePaola, and Maurice Sendak, writing books characterized by a "hushed contemplation of aloneness and connection" that functions as both queer subtext and powerful evocation of childhood struggles with attachment and separation (Green 2019). And, like Sendak, Lobel, and many others, Brown was edited by Ursula Nordstrom, herself a lesbian, who Jesse Green describes as "drawn to the intensity of feeling that the closet aroused" in some authors' work.

The latent queerness of Brown's shapeshifting bunny is brought to the fore in non-binary graphic artist Maia Kobabe's retelling, *The Nonbinary Bunny*.[7] In this reimagined take on the story, the bunny is explaining to eir mother what it means to be non-binary through a series of imagined transformations that resist the stable identity categories the mother longs to place the child into. In the end, the stability of her maternal love is established not by the bunny returning to eir original form, but by the mother affirming eir transformations: "Whether you are a sunrise, or a frog, or a cat, or a bird, I am still your mother. I will support you wherever you go" (2019). Kobabe's reimagined conclusion breaks open the closeted impulse of the original to offer a triumphantly queer reinterpretation in which a child's transformations are not only imagined or metaphorical, but sometimes literal. What the original and this reimagining share is a longing for freedom and safety, to break away and still be held.

My other favourite children's book has a decidedly less cozy aesthetic but continues to focus on the safety of the home, a recurring theme in books for young children. *Lizzy's Lion* is a 1984 story by Canadian poet Dennis Lee, illustrated by Marie-Louise Gay. Lee was a poet first, winning the Governor General's Award for his collection *Civil Elegies and Other Poems* (1972). Shortly afterward he published his best-known book of poems for children, *Alligator Pie* (1974), a collection that critics have argued shares his other poetry's concern with "Canada's colonized condition and...the need to become a full citizen," a process that begins with "reclaiming language and liberating imagination" in childhood (Sorfleet 2008). Writing children's poems rooted in Canadian places and activities, in the mundane day-to-day of Canadian children's lives put Lee's work in conversation with the larger concerns of forging a distinct national culture in Canada following the Second World War. And while *Lizzy's Lion* has very little to say about Canada explicitly, it is certainly rooted in the details of a child's life.

As with *The Runaway Bunny*, my copy is inscribed with the year 1986, but this inscription was written by my brother, who would have been five at the time, in the uneven block letters of a child. *Lizzy's Lion* has much of Lee's characteristic irreverence and, like his other children's books, is written in rhyming verse. The text is embedded in boxes on a series of double-spread, full colour images, functioning almost like captions to the illustrated narrative. The story is about a girl, Lizzy, who keeps a lion in her bedroom. One night a robber breaks into Lizzy's room to steal her piggy bank; when he encounters the lion, the robber attempts to befriend the animal with candy, but the lion is uninterested. In a classic fairy-tale device, the lion can only be persuaded if his correct name is used, which the robber tries but fails to identify (the name is Lion; you'd think he'd have tried that one). Because of this failure, the lion eats the robber, and Lizzy wakes up in time to tidy up the body parts, put them in the garbage, and return to bed.

Compared to the sweet pastoral aesthetic of *The Runaway Bunny*, *Lizzy's Lion* is a snuff film of a book, but a commonality leaps out to me: Lizzy and her lion's violence are justified by the violation of the domestic sphere, where Lizzy reigns, much as the mother bunny's proper sphere is the domestic space of the burrow, where her child must ultimately return to. On the one hand, subversion is followed quickly by a return to the status quo, with Lizzy and her lion viewed through her bedroom window cozily asleep in a scene reminiscent of mother and bunny tucked into their burrow. On the other hand, the queer and radical possibilities implied by the child's violence and the presence of the sleeping lion with the robber's decapitated head in the garbage can (a mere scrap of fabric in the illustration), remain just under the surface of that conclusion. Where do these possibilities point us—toward the complicity of white women in upholding a violent, carceral state in the name of keeping some of us and our cozy domestic spaces safe from the perceived threat of outsiders? Or to a queer fantasy of women and girls' liberation from the violence of masculinity via the embrace of subversive resistance? Can these two readings be disentangled? *Should* they be?

As I grew, my interest in reading about women navigating the smallness of their domestic spheres remained: *Pride and Prejudice, Little Women*, and *An Old-Fashioned Girl* are all books concerned, in different ways, with how women operate within and chafe against the limitations of the small worlds they are confined within. The whiteness of these women and their relative wealth registered to me as a young reader only insofar as I was able to identify with them seamlessly, to imagine myself in their schoolrooms, parlours, and carriages with no more of an empathetic leap than was required by annual class visits to Upper Canada Village, where costumed historical interpreters taught us to churn butter. This is not reading for difference but for sameness, and for the pleasure of seeing yourself echoed everywhere, through time and space; it's a search for what is now disparagingly referred to as "relatability." Reading for difference wasn't a skill I would learn until much later in my education, one that required me to put aside my instinctive emotional responses to texts in favour of trying to understand the work they were doing in their original contexts. As a young reader, though, I was hungry for the opportunity to imagine myself into the stories I read. Reading these stories married the unthinking pleasures of my own universality with early lessons in gendered limitations; I could see myself everywhere, but everywhere I saw myself I was constrained (I picture, again, the bunny imagining himself into a thousand transformations without ever leaving the safety of the burrow). At the same time, the sentimental and romantic novels I loved recentred these women characters in their constrained domestic spaces by focusing on the things that concerned them: their relationships with their sisters and mothers, the books they read and the letters they wrote, and above all, the feelings they felt, feelings that consistently guided the moral compasses of the novels.

This tension between constraint and liberation is evident in Louisa May Alcott's *Little Women*. Based roughly on Alcott's own childhood, *Little Women* tells the story of the March sisters coming of age against the backdrop of the American Civil War. It follows protagonist Jo March as she matures from an impetuous tomboy to a married woman and mother. This was the conventional form of the period in which Alcott was writing—the 1850s and 60s, contemporary to Stowe—and the genre conventions she was working within. But whereas Stowe is described as harnessing these conventions to make a political argument, Alcott is generally understood to be subverting them to extend, however minutely, the imagined possibilities for women's lives (I will be a bird; I will have a lion...).

*Little Women* was published in two volumes in 1868 and 1869. By this point in her life (her late thirties), Alcott was a feminist and abolitionist, and had established herself as a writer of gothic and sensationalist stories for popular magazines. *Little Women* was her first foray into writing for girls, a genre that she was originally hesitant to try. Writing for girls was beginning to coalesce into a recognizable genre in the mid-nineteenth century, and was characterized by a series of sentimental conventions, with the heroine's narrative offering "a map for the imaginative journey toward the possibility of control—not over life, a manifestly impossible task, but over the self and its responses to life's vicissitudes" (Campbell 1994, 119). The sentimental heroine often began as a self-indulgent and irresponsible child, before maturing into a practical and responsible young woman ready to take control of her own domestic sphere; within these novels we can see how sentimentalism becomes a technology for training white middle-class women to take their proper place within the nation, via their responsibility for the management of the domestic sphere and the moral education of children. Alcott's best-known novels follow these conventions—she was, after all, trying to make money by tapping into a popular new market—but as is the case with many examples of genre fiction that stood the test of time, she approaches the conventions with some subversive differences.

In the essay "Pure Heroines," Jia Tolentino ponders how different the narrative possibilities are for girls than they are for women. Discussing the busy industriousness of the female heroines she loved—Anne Shirley, Hermione Granger, Harriet the Spy—she wonders if "part of the reason these childhood characters are all so independent, so eager to make the most of whatever presents itself" is that "they—or, more to the point, their creators—understand that adulthood is always looming, which means marriage and children, which means, in effect, the end" (2019, 102). Similarly, Wendy Roy points out that the authors of sentimental girls' stories—such as Lucy Maud Montgomery's series of "Anne" books—often extended their protagonists' childhoods, delaying the stultifying domestic narratives that seemed to inevitably attend adulthood and marriage, with the expected arrival at an emotional maturity that turned every puckish girl into a Marmee (2019). While Alcott found her greatest success working within the genre of sentimental books for girls, with its expected convention of white women's lives moving inevitably toward marriage and children, she rejected that path in her own life. Alcott remained unmarried and childless, and she is often quoted as saying, "I am more than half-persuaded that I am a man's soul put by some freak of nature into a woman's body ... because I have fallen in love with so many pretty girls and never once the least bit with any man."[8] Alcott's feminism and queerness come into tension with her practical approach to writing as a career, and her attention to the desires of her publishers and readers.

This tension comes through most clearly in the contentious conclusion of the second part of *Little Women*, when Jo marries not her childhood best friend Laurie, but a much older German man, Professor Bhaer. Scholar of nineteenth-century women's writing Donna M. Campbell describes this conclusion as a deliberate subversion; in Alcott's own words, "'Jo' should have remained a literary spinster but so many enthusiastic young ladies wrote to me clamorously demanding that she should marry Laurie, or somebody, that I didn't dare to refuse & out of perversity went & made a funny match for her" (qtd. in Campbell 1994, 124). By pairing Jo with Professor Bhaer, Alcott follows the letter of the sentimental novel while rejecting the spirit, creating a happy ending that is emotionally disappointing and thus refusing sentimentality's insistence that every woman's story is moving inevitably toward a fulfilling marriage.

This resistant tension in the conclusion of *Little Women* is brought to the forefront in Greta Gerwig's 2019 film adaptation, which shows us another woman storyteller grappling with these same problems: how to unfold a female *Bildungsroman* that doesn't end in the narrative death that is the fully matured sentimental heroine. Gerwig tackles this problem via two key transformations, both of which have been alternately praised for their boldness and critiqued for changing the beloved original. First, she plays with the chronology of the story, blurring the first and second parts of the novel by moving back and forth between the March sisters as grown women and as girls in a way that layers the warmth and vitality of their childhood scenes into the more severe adult narrative, while also offering an implicit critique of how adulthood has curtailed them. When we see an adult Meg, for example, berating herself for the indulgence of fabric for a new dress—a trope of the sentimental heroine maturing via control over the self and increased practicality—we are encouraged to read it against her childish pleasure in beautiful things, and perhaps to ask whether one Meg is more fully formed than the other. Gerwig also adds a frame narrative to her adaptation that overtly comments on the constraining expectations of Alcott's publishers and readers, and how those expectations mirrored the constrained possibilities for women's own lives. In this frame we see Jo March negotiating a publishing contract for a book that is also *Little Women*; her negotiations particularly centre on the plot detail of whether Jo will settle down with a romantic interest in the end. Frame narrative Jo at first refuses, but ultimately bows to the expectations of her publisher—and by extension her readers—by having textual Jo declare her love for Professor Bhaer. In the disjunction between these two conclusions—one focused on domestic security, with Jo marrying and starting a school, and the other refusing domesticity in favour of her creative and professional goals in a way that matches Alcott's own biography—the movie lays bare how generic expectations shape narratives and lives, not only delineating what kinds of stories can be told, but also curtailing how we imagine our own possibilities. After all, if narratives work as a kind of theory, a way of structuring and making sense of the world, then they can also be coercive.

What's striking about the feminist intervention of Gerwig's adaptation is that it doesn't diminish textual Jo's choices by framing them *as* textual; instead, the final scene of Jo surrounded by her family and friends is joyous and celebratory, a sun-soaked picnic afternoon that looks much more like the film's childhood scenes than its drab visions of adulthood. This conclusion leans into the spirit of the sentimental novel, in which grown women become most fully realized by creating their own warm and loving domestic spheres. The frame narrative, on the other hand, is more grimly lit, focused on the material production of Jo's book. The juxtaposition of these scenes doesn't suggest one is better than the other, but rather points out that one is the product of the other. Images of the physical book being printed, compiled, and bound remind us that sentimental narratives are an act of creative and physical labour as well as economic realities, with the picturesque pleasures of the March family relying on a hidden infrastructure that imagines them into existence. We might, as readers of this film, even go so far as to interpret this frame narrative as a critique of white middle-class femininity as a fantastical construction upheld by often racialized labour made invisible, an impossible fantasy that is all the more dangerous for its coercive appeal.

These are the interpretations of a mature reader bringing years of training to bear on familiar texts. But for my childhood self, they offered a queer and feminist education, as well as a racial one. *The Runaway Bunny* taught me that I was inherently worthy of care, that my dreams and my dignity mattered, even—or especially—if they were out of step with what the world wanted for me. That I was malleable, able to change, but that my transformations had to be managed by a mother's love. *Lizzy's Lion* taught me that I was vulnerable, but also capable of violence; that my violence was, perhaps, justified by or even celebrated because of my vulnerability. And *Little Women* taught me that white girls occupied curtailed worlds built for us by white men, but that imagination and pluck could liberate us from those worlds, or at least allow us to carve out small spaces for ourselves within them. It taught me that queerness was as thrilling as it was narratively impossible. These are truths that I have spent much of my life, as a reader and a feminist, struggling to reconcile.

In "Unmasking Criticism: The Problem with Being a Good Reader of Sentimental Rhetoric," feminist literary critic Faye Halpern asks what it means "for a critic to be implicated (as opposed to merely caught up) in what she studies," and why it is that sentimentality in particular tends to make critics feel implicated (2011, 52). As Halpern explains, the general critical attitude toward sentimental rhetoric is one of contempt; marked as it is by conventionality, sentimental rhetoric seems to demand a critical approach that unmasks the text's real motivations, whether they're suspect or subversive (2011, 55). But that distanced and disdainful reading is at odds with feminist interventions into how literary and cultural criticism might be done, via forms that are "less compulsive, aggressive, lonely, competitive; more communal, caring, and integrated with love and politics" (Ascher et al. 1984, xxii). Taking sentimental texts seriously becomes an entry point for putting ourselves and our feelings back into our criticism, not dividing them off, but seeing that what moves us is what we should be paying attention to.

Sentimental stories gave me a theoretical framework for making sense of my own life; revisiting those stories now, as an adult, lets me make a different kind of sense out of them. I was hungry then to see myself in what I read because it gave my experiences a container, and I was all too eager to toss aside those parts of myself that I could not find in my favourite stories. There was no space for fat girls there, and so I learned to understand my fatness as a mistake, something I would eventually overcome as I transformed into my true self. These stories gave me hope that one day I would get myself under control.

As I return to them now, I feel the impulse not to reject them, for all their troubled histories, but to explore their queer slippages and attend to what, in their contexts of production, was unsayable. I take comfort in Kobabe's non-binary bunny and Gerwig's queer Jo, not because their interpretations redeem these stories' sentimentality, but because they make me feel like we're figuring something out together.

What excites me about reading is the process of interpreting and discussing, of visiting and revisiting a significant story and bringing our whole selves to bear, personally and collectively, on the problem of meaning. It's in that endless and transformative process that I find a way forward, through the entangled paths of reading for sameness and difference, of reading to learn and unlearn. These sentimental narratives have been part of my education, and I feel deeply implicated in them. But I am also implicated in the palimpsestic way I have come to read them, through my own histories and increasingly in dialogue with the readings of others. I'm not trying to decide if sentimental stories are good or bad. I want to dwell, instead, in the gloriously messy process of collective meaning-making.

# CARING
# FEROCIOUSLY

**MEANING IS A THING I MAKE WITH OTHERS.**
I think I've known this for a long time, since the moment my
mother told me she was going to die and I felt myself launched
into space, tether snapped, free-floating. A feminist ethics of
care insists that we are not autonomous, liberal subjects but are
constituted by our kinships, our networks of relation. We are
who we care for, and who cares for us. I've learned about kinship from Indigenous thinkers pushing back against the eugeni-
cist understandings of identity and belonging propagated by
the settler colonial state as it strives to eliminate Indigeneity
by reducing it to who has which genes. As Sisseton Wahpeton
Oyate scholar Kim TallBear has explained, the "rapacious
individualism" of the settler colonial project was at the root
of white settlers' profound failure to understand relationality:

"The whites did not know how to do kinship" (2016). The fetishization of individualism and autonomy is also endemic to academia. You can see it in how we treat collaboration, credit, hierarchies of labour, and ideas of innovation. "Publish or perish" sometimes feels like a literal threat: make a name for yourself, or you'll cease to exist.

There are a lot of different ways to tell the story of who I am, and these days I'm most well-versed in the academic genres, CVs and "career narrative" documents crafted for the review and tenure process, deeply conventional genres of life-writing that strip the personal out and leave little, if any, space for registering our kinships and communities. The Social Sciences and Humanities Research Council of Canada encourages us to delineate "special circumstances" such as "child-rearing" and "illness or disability"—the parts of our non-academic selves that might insidiously creep into the life of the mind we're supposed to be living exclusively. Within the constraints of these genres, I have struggled to articulate or even understand the relationship between my academic and non-academic selves, while the indivisibility of those selves has become increasingly central to my understanding of feminist scholarship and of, in the words of scholar of Black Geographies Katherine McKittrick, where I know from.[1]

I want to try my hand at telling a different kind of story, and I need to begin by telling you a few things about Teresa Joan Penner, my mother, who went by Terry. She was the second youngest of five children. Her mother was an English war bride and her father a Mennonite farm boy-turned-RAF bomber-turned-soil scientist. I don't think it was a happy household, and my mother wanted the family she created to be happy. She threw herself with great conviction into the business of domestic joy.

She left home when she was young, taught herself to cook by asking the Italian and Portuguese women who shopped at the grocery store where she worked about the things they were buying, things she'd never seen before: artichokes, arugula, eggplants, and hard, spicy sausages. She met my father at university, and she chose him, and she never stopped choosing him. Her love was a vise, sometimes overwhelming but always firm.

As an adult she was loud and unabashedly feminist, didn't shave her legs or armpits, never wore high heels, grew her own medicine in her garden, paid the neighbourhood kids five cents a tadpole to populate the pond she dug herself. I can still picture her waist-deep in that hole, sweating and grinning. I inherited her grin—all teeth. She gave me a copy of *Our Bodies, Ourselves* when I hit puberty. She gave me a Blessing Way—a ceremony welcoming me into womanhood—when I had my first period (I still have the clay goddess she made me, marked in reddish brown glaze with the thumbprints of all the women there). She asked me about masturbation. We sat in front of a mirror together and looked at our vulvas.

She, my feminist mother, Teresa Joan Penner (who went by Terry), did not believe in queerness. She thought it was a phase (for me, as she believed it had been for her). She wanted to know why there wasn't a straight pride parade. She wanted me to lose weight so badly, so that I could be happy. When I was in the second grade she took me to a specialist to find out why I was so fat; I was an active kid, played outside, ate the healthy meals she made for me, and the doctor could offer no explanation for the problem that was my body. She tried to be okay with my fatness after that, to teach me that I was beautiful and valuable, that my body was a goddess's body, but she kept looking for explanations, for stories that would make sense of me. Not long before she died, she went to visit some friends in Vermont, and came back with a new theory: that my fatness was my body shielding me from the trauma of her illness. I learned to experience my fatness and my queerness as barriers between myself and happiness, psychic padding I had put in place because I was too frightened to reach for what I really wanted. I did my best, for years after her death, to become the person I thought she had wanted me to be, brave and fierce, thin and straight.

It's so unfair how someone, once dead, is frozen in their opinions. She would have changed her mind a thousand times by now, I am certain.

She loved us, my father and my brother and me, fiercely and completely, and she was also dedicated to her friendships with other women, friendships built around mutual networks of care, the exchange of food and clothes and childcare. She believed in the value of women, the strength of women, the world-building magic of women. Her friend Agi, my godmother, was fifteen years her senior, and had lived through the 1956 Hungarian Revolution. Agi told us stories about eating the horses that had been shot in the street, and she liked to drink whipping cream by the glass. I learned from Agi about how trauma lives on in the body, her desire for rich foods a way of feeding her starving child self. My mother's friend Faith was an Indigenous woman who trained German Shepherds and taught my mother to smudge; I remember being invited over to eat the first rabbit her son Noah had trapped, not quite understanding the significance but knowing I'd been invited into something important. Terry's friends were Mad and disabled and poor and racialized, musicians, poets, and healers. In the final years of her life she was also Mad and disabled, and taught me how to ask permission before touching someone's wheelchair, how to hold my arm still and strong to support someone who's in pain. I am still learning the lessons in radical care that my mother taught me. Those lessons were not about moral purity, but political ferocity. During the final years of her life, my mother adopted the pseudonym "the ferocious one-breasted woman." She would rip up those signs people put on their lawns warning that they've been sprayed with pesticides, writing notes about the links between pesticides and cancer, signing them with her new moniker. She told me once about a sculpture she was imagining (she never got the chance to make it): a woman stands with a hole blasted through her torso where her breast used to be; her rib cage is intact, but you can see right through her. All the soft tissue is gone, leaving only bone and emptiness. Ferocity, I now believe, can be a form of care; ferocity is a way of caring so much about the world that you refuse to stop fighting for it.

I am not a naturally radical thinker, a fact that I think disappointed my mother, who was. She wanted me to be a risk-taker, more fearless, even scrappy. I think she felt herself to be a little out of step with the world, and knew something of what being out of step might expose about how the world is built. That is what I mean by radical: looking at the world as a set of systems that need to be changed, not accepted. As a child, I was comforted by systems. I liked getting good grades and being praised. To temper my aversion to pain, my mother enrolled me in horseback riding lessons, which I kept up until she got too sick to drive me to the barn. She tried to convince me to climb trees, jump in rivers, learn to throw a ball. In contrast I wanted to learn calligraphy, write sad poems, and also be in charge of every game. I liked to play school with my friends; I was always the teacher. I was comforted by rules and certain that, if I could just find the right set and follow them to the letter, my life would unfold with the predictable grace of the stories I'd grown up loving.

My mother died when I was sixteen, and our small family splintered apart without her; her mother, my grandmother Joan, died three years later, further rupturing my relationship with my extended family, until I felt adrift in the world, a lost girl with no idea who I wanted to be. In a sentimental narrative this is probably where a man two decades my senior would arrive to provide me with a stern moral education and, eventually, children to keep my busy mind occupied. But being a modern woman, I found another source of structure, stability, and comfort.

Academia was the perfect escape for a smart, fat, broken white girl who was already committed to turning experiences into ideas so that I could hold them at a distance. Academia taught me the next step: turning ideas into accomplishments that would help me build a new sense of self, a new identity that lay first in grades, and later in grants, publications, and awards. Many of the rules in academe are tacit, requiring a particular kind of attention to observe and follow them, thus rewarding those of us who—by virtue of class, race, and prior educational experience—arrived already trained to read these social cues. And those who are "in the club" continue to be rewarded for playing by the rules. The interpolating force of the university draws its acolytes in, convincing us that we are on the side of the institution. It seizes upon the language of radical scholarship and turns it into a further justification for the power of the university. As Fred Moten and Stefano Harney explain in "The University and the Undercommons: Seven Theses," no amount of questioning and critiquing the university will actually dismantle its oppressive structures, because critique is the function of the university professional and can only enhance the profession, never undermine it (2004, 111). This world of rigid hierarchies and structured languages of critique is the world I brought my ongoing search for theories into, to help me make sense of things. I latched onto academic work so I could move *away* from the hard, embodied lessons my mother taught me, and into what I thought would be a more manageable realm of disembodied ideas.

I don't believe that theory always leads us away from lived experience; in fact, theory can often lead us back into our experiences, giving us a new way to understand them. But theory can also be a form of dissociation, like my mother's theory that my fatness was a sign of trauma, a theory that cut me off from my body for years. In retrospect, it doesn't surprise me that, during my PhD—specifically the year of my comprehensive exams—I began to lose weight. A dangerous amount of weight, in fact. I don't remember how it began, but one day I found I couldn't eat the foods I used to. Almost everything hurt, stabbing pains in my stomach that would leave me on the floor, curled up in the fetal position. I was put through a barrage of medical tests looking for viruses, bacterial infections, or abscesses, but there was nothing physically wrong with me.

To address this mysterious ailment I started trying fad diets, raw food and week-long juice fasts, and I kept losing weight at a remarkable rate. Through all of this I continued to push my body with hours of hot yoga, bike rides, and hikes. I became obsessed with how few calories I could eat in a day and still function, getting up in the morning and biking to the office for a full day of comps reading before heading to yoga and home for a dinner of kale juice or vegan protein powder mixed with water. I was in pain all the time, exhausted all the time, disappearing before my own eyes, and I was ecstatic. God, I had wanted to be thin so fucking badly, but I'd never been the type to wear away in grief, to take to my bed and refuse meals. Now, at last, I was *becoming her*—that deeply feeling yet stoic, sentimental heroine. And I was praised for it, for disappearing, and especially for working through it. My supervisor noted my relentless work ethic. Everyone else noticed my shrinking body. I started to be able to shop at the same stores as my friends. I was suffering, and I was proud of myself for doing so, because through this suffering I was becoming the person I thought my mother had wanted me to be. Heck, I even dabbled in dating men.

And then I got better. The yoga was helping with stress reduction, and successfully completing my comprehensive exams helped even more. Slowly my gut started to heal, and my appetite returned, ferociously. I wanted food again, and hated myself for it. My doctor praised my weight gain, telling me it was a sign of healing. Later I would treasure this reminder that, for my body, health and fatness correspond. But at the time all I knew was that I had failed, again, to be *that* woman. I fell into cycles of yo-yo dieting, restrictive eating, and compulsive late-night bingeing, but couldn't find my way back to that girl with no appetite. It was too late; I was hungry again.

I can remember the day that I decided to stop dieting. I was in Edmonton by then; I had, at my stepmother's encouragement, been living on a keto diet alongside a regimen of regular hot yoga, and I'd been losing weight again, had just barely managed to buy a suit for my first campus interview at a straight-sized clothing store. I spent so many hours thinking about food, obsessing about food, but in the meantime, I'd started to read some fat theorists and fat activists, and to ponder the radical idea that being fat might be okay. I remember borrowing my first fat studies book—Esther Rothblum and Sondra Solovay's *The Fat Studies Reader*—from the university library and sneaking it home, buried under other books. I didn't even read it that first time, it felt too dangerous. When I eventually started reading fat studies scholarship, I learned that the fat liberation movement came out of radical lesbian feminist organizing of the 1970s with the work of The Fat Underground, which targeted not self-esteem but institutionalized medical fatphobia. Unlike the contemporary whitewashed "body positivity" movement, fat liberation recognized that fat is not only a feminist issue, as Susie Orbach famously said, but also "a queer issue, and a racialized issue, and an issue of class—because fatness is inseparable from all other intersections of identity" (qtd. in Simon 2019). Thinking of my fatness as part of my identity rather than a problem to be solved was an inherently radicalizing experience for me, not just as I learned to reject diet culture and its stranglehold on my time and energy, but also as I learned to see the entanglement of my own liberation with the liberation of Black and Indigenous people, disabled people, working-class people, and chronically ill people.

Learning to be at home in my fat body has also been a fundamental part of learning to feel the grief and trauma of my mother's death: I could not do one without first doing the other. It has made me less polite and fearful, less prone to following rules now that I'm enthusiastically breaking one great big one. It has helped me to become the radical thinker I believe my mother *actually* wanted me to be. I am working to embrace the queer and feminist politics of radical softness, a term coined by artist Lora Mathis via a series of artworks shared on their Tumblr. In a 2015 interview in *Hooligan Magazine,* they describe it as "the idea that unapologetically sharing your emotions is a political move" as well as "a way to combat the societal idea that feelings are a sign of weakness" (qtd. in McLean 2015). Mathis's phrase 'RADICAL SOFTNESS AS A WEAPON' strikes me as a powerful way to reconceptualize the beauty of fat bodies, embracing their capacious softness as well as their disruptiveness. It is also part of a longer queer feminist tradition of linking care to radical politics, one that is perhaps best expressed by Black lesbian feminist poet Audre Lorde's concept of self-care as warfare.

Lorde's linking of self-care to warfare is an idea too often quoted out of context, particularly as neo-liberalism has industrialized and packaged self-care in the twenty-first century. The phrase comes from the epilogue to Lorde's 1988 essay collection *A Burst of Light,* in which she connects her experiences of living with cancer to other fights for liberation. She writes, "Overextending myself is not stretching myself. I had to accept how difficult it is to monitor the difference. Necessary for me as cutting down on sugar. Crucial. Physically. Psychically. Caring for myself is not self-indulgence, it is self-preservation, and that is an act of political warfare" (Lorde 1988, 130). Lorde is writing specifically about self-preservation as a Black lesbian feminist, the refusal to be either forced to live or allowed to die.[2] She refuses the violent insistence upon survival at all costs promulgated by the healthcare industry: "I try to weave my life-prolonging treatments into a living context—to resist giving myself over like a sacrificial offering to the furious, single-minded concentration upon cure that leaves no room to examine what living and fighting on a physical front can mean" (1988, 131). In this way, Lorde's work makes me think of my mother's defiant death, her choice to die by suicide rather than undergoing endless radiation and chemotherapy treatments in the face of a terminal diagnosis.

Sara Ahmed describes Lorde's refusal to fixate on cure as a refusal of "self-care [as] a technique of governance: the duty to care for one's self often written as a duty to care for one's own happiness, flourishing, well-being" (2014), linking it to the refusal to prioritize individual happiness over collective justice. Continuing to contextualize self-care as rooted in Black lesbian feminist thought, Ahmed also points to how it might be extended to ideas about sustaining various forms of "fragile communities" that "reassemble ourselves through the ordinary, everyday and often painstaking work of looking after ourselves; looking after each other" (2014). Refusing cure also recalls the transformative work of disability justice scholars like Eli Clare who, in *Brilliant Imperfection: Grappling with Cure*, pushes back against the idea that cure is always the goal, with disability being a kind of brokenness that must be either fixed or eliminated. From the perspective of disability justice, we can see how the obsession with cure is about throwing aside those bodies that don't satisfy the demands of capitalism, that aren't useful enough.

At the intersection of Black feminist thought and disability justice, I also locate the work of Tricia Hersey, known as The Nap Bishop. Hersey's project, *The Nap Ministry*, seeks to dismantle white supremacy and capitalism by embracing rest as a form of resistance. Like Mathis's 'RADICAL SOFTNESS AS A WEAPON' and Lorde's self-care as warfare, rest as resistance is an example of radical negativity, an approach to transformative social justice that identifies the subversive potential in maligned values and practices (Gorman 2019). Saying that it is good to be soft, to care for ourselves, and to rest is a rejection of the capitalist fetishization of work, the white supremacist reduction of Black bodies to their labour potential, and the patriarchal disdain for feminized qualities such as care and gentleness. But these framings are not only about valuing softness, care, and rest— they also recognize the subversive potential that lies within these forms of refusal. Softness, care, and rest can be, counterintuitively, sites of rage, refusal, and ferocity.

Fatness can also be a form of radical softness. The aesthetics of fatness, in which we reclaim how beautiful our fat bodies are, celebrating our dimpled skin and abundant rolls, also reclaims what it means to be soft in a world that demands we are constantly hard, especially on ourselves. Fat theory, like queer theory, was an entry point for me into theory that put me back into my body and feelings, instead of moving me away from them. But softness and self-care can also be a way out, for white people, an excuse not to do the hard work of dismantling white supremacy until we feel like it.[3] As Twitter user @dumb_dyke_tears aptly summarized:

for a lot of white queers (esp those who are mentally ill) the entire concept of 'self-care' becomes a stagnation point where we never move beyond seeking our own comfort. but when white people prioritize our own comfort over all else, it inevitably leads to white supremacy.

The belief that self-care is inherently valuable because it centres the stigmatized and feminized qualities of emotionality and softness, has its roots in sentimentality. It speaks to sentimentality's positioning of white women as the moral driver of the nation, whose role is to stay out of the direct action of politics while still guiding the collective in the direction of moral purity. It also speaks to the neo-liberal redeployment of sentimentality in the twenty-first century that frames care as a deeply individualized activity usually mediated by institutions or corporations. Radical softness, as Andi Schwartz argues in a *GUTS Magazine* article on "The Cultural Politics of Softness," is only as radical as the change it makes and the world it builds (2018). Hersey's rest and Lorde's self-care are subversive because they are about the survival of Black women and their communities, because it allows them to survive, resist, and create in a world designed to kill them. My own softness is not inherently radical, but I can make it into a weapon if I point it in the right direction. Ferocious care, my mother's tool for facing the world, has become central to my own articulation of a queer feminist ethics of care.

On November 20, 2016, I wrote a Facebook post marking the sixteenth anniversary of Teresa Joan Penner's death, an anniversary that also marked the moment when she had been dead for more of my life than she had been alive. I wrote:

My mother was abrasive. She was loud. She loved people with all of her heart and her body and her voice. She screamed and cried and fought because the world was always worth that energy, because what she believed in was always worth defending. And throughout all that fighting, and all that suffering, she maintained a great well of tenderness within her.

In that moment, I made a commitment to fight as hard as she did, and with as much tenderness. It is a commitment I am still trying to fulfill, as I rethink what it means to tell the story of myself as a feminist, and as a woman who is fat and white, queer and asexual. I know now that I can reject the version of happiness she envisioned for me, that I *must* reject it if I want to live my life with the same ferocity that she did. But I'm tired of pretending that her love and her loss aren't as central to the scholar, feminist, and human I've become as any of the other lines on my CV. There is a hole blasted straight through me, like the sculpture she once envisioned; what a relief it is to finally tell you about it.

# #RELATABLE

REASSERTING THE SELF IN SCHOLARLY WORK IS A FEMINIST intervention into the patriarchal ideal of disembodied and objective knowledge. And like all feminist interventions, it has been met by multiple forms of backlash, from accusations of neo-liberal fixation on individual experience to implications that it's "dumbing down" or reducing the intellectual sophistication of scholarly work. Or, to put this another way: it makes me feel vulnerable to try to bring my "self" into my work like this, even though this writing gets closer to what I actually want to say than any of the more conventional work I've done. And while I am certainly drawing on the feminist tradition of autotheory—which blurs the lines between theory and autobiography, and between work and self—I am also getting in touch with my own discursive roots. I may have been raised on sentimental stories, but I came of age amid the explosive rise of social media and Web 2.0's favourite genre: the personal essay.[1]

Sharing often banal personal stories is built into the fabric of web publishing, from chat rooms and blogs to social media and online publications that distinguished themselves via their hot takes and personalized framings. Former *Jezebel* blogger Jia Tolentino opens her book of essays, *Trick Mirror*, with a brief history of writing for the Internet, beginning with her personalized Angelfire subpage, complete with *Dawson's Creek* JPEGs, animated GIFs, and favourite song lyrics. "In 1999," she insists, "it felt different to spend all day on the Internet. This was true for everyone, not just for ten-year-olds" (2019, 4). My own memories of the early Internet were similarly idyllic. As a child I used a boxy grey Macintosh Classic to write long, unfinished stories about magical horses; when we first got dial-up I was an active member of a *Reboot* forum dedicated to discussions of the Canadian animated series about characters who lived inside a computer. By the time I hit thirteen, I was active on a risqué Madonna chat room, where I posed as a sixteen-year-old and flirted with strangers. I quickly became versed in the freedoms the Internet offered me, a chance to perform other selves outside the restrictions of my family and school.

That sense of the Internet as a space of performative freedom shifted with the arrival of Facebook, which for me also aligned with a year spent studying abroad, my first time living away from Ottawa. The transformations of the decade leading up to Facebook's emergence, as Tolentino outlines them, were powered by the increasingly social dimensions of Web 2.0: "Through the emergence of blogging, personal lives were becoming public domain, and social incentives—to be liked, to be seen—were becoming economic ones. The mechanisms of Internet exposure began to seem like a viable foundation for a career...The Internet, in promising a potentially unlimited audience, began to seem like the natural home of self-expression" (2019, 6-7). In 2007, the social Internet was how I stayed connected to friends and family back home, and then to the friends I'd made abroad, and then to the new networks I made when I went off to grad school. My sense of the Internet as a space of performative freedom shifted to a pressing concern with performing a consistent and recognizable self for these various publics and communities—a concern that escalated once I entered grad school and began, however hesitantly, to build a career as an academic. I got a Twitter account, then eventually a personal website; I was not trying to monetize my self-expression directly, but I was actively working to professionalize myself, and the Internet as a site of active and continuous self-performance began to play a central role in how I articulated myself as a scholar and thinker.

I'm not quite sure how I arrived at the reversal where the self I performed online felt more authentically me than the one I occupied in "real life," but it had a lot to do with my shifting relationship to my career. In 2009, when I created my Twitter account at the University of Victoria's Digital Humanities Summer Institute, I was in the grip of imposter syndrome, desperately pretending to be someone who was supposed to be in intellectual and academic spaces. Everyone around me, it seemed, occupied the role of the intellectual with ease; they knew how to dress, what drink to order at the bar, what kinds of small talk would make them sound professional and interesting, but not too big for their grad-student britches (or Reitman's pencil skirts). What looked natural for others felt like a shoddy disguise on me, one I was sure someone would see through eventually. By 2015, when I started making my first podcast, *Witch, Please*, I was doing my imitation of an intellectual on a daily basis, in classrooms, department meetings, wine receptions, and job interviews; I'd become well versed in laughing along and looking up the reference later. I was performing my own intellectualism so regularly, in fact, that it had stopped feeling like a performance—right up until I began the podcast, and was surprised to discover a different version of me. My podcasting self felt authentic from the start, largely because on the podcast I was emboldened to say the very things that felt unsayable in other professional contexts. The more I said those things out loud—the more I named my embodied experiences, emotional reactions, silliness and messiness and uncertainty— the more uncomfortably aware I became of how ill-fitting my academic performance had always been. Who knows if I was fooling anyone else; I certainly was not fooling myself.

I don't mean to claim that I found my true self on *Witch, Please*. Rather, the opportunity to perform my expertise otherwise highlighted what had not been working for me in conventional academic culture. I found, in grad school and beyond, that I had a knack for debate and argumentation; surrounded by people who engaged with one another's ideas combatively, tearing their opponents down to establish their own intellectual worth, I had learned to tear down and one-up with the best of them. But I didn't realize how little I enjoyed this aggressive approach until I tried something different, a pleasurable and collaborative feminist conversation with joy and accountability, rather than winning, at its heart. The question wasn't whether this version of myself was more truly *me* than the version I'd been performing previously; I just liked this podcasting Hannah a whole lot more.

The online self, as scholars of life-writing Sidonie Smith and Julia Watson explain in "Virtually Me: A Toolbox about Online Self-Presentation," is not stable but mediated and provisional, and some online spaces value the performance of authenticity more than others. While some forums might have norms of anonymity, others expect transparency and consistency. This is particularly true of influencer culture, where generating what Smith and Watson call an "aura of authenticity" is highly valued (2014, 76). Influencers' ability to monetize their various feeds is dependent on building a consistent brand that their followers trust.[2] Influencers are authentic, consistent, and above all relatable—just like us, but better. That authenticity is neither real nor fake: it's just another performance of the self. When we let go of the belief that social media can be a path to, or revelation of, personal authenticity, then we can ask different, more productive questions about our activity online, such as: what kinds of behaviours do these media encourage, and how do they make us feel?

For Tolentino, the answer seems to be: not good. Her conclusions about the present and future of the Internet are grim, to put it mildly. Social media is addictive and numbing, coercing us into producing truly wild hot takes in the interests of maintaining our relevance and visibility, while also inundating us with "fire hoses of information" until we become incapable of distinguishing "the banal from the profound" (Tolentino 2019, 30–31). And, because our attention, data, and political radicalization continue to be highly profitable for large media corporations, it's only going to get worse. As she concludes, "[c]apitalism has no land left to cultivate but the self. Everything is being cannibalized—not just goods and labor, but personality and relationships and attention" (2019, 33). The recourse for someone like Tolentino, who built her career on blogs and websites like *The Hairpin* and *Jezebel*, lies in her approach to writing in *Trick Mirror*, in which she contemplates "the spheres of public imagination that have shaped [her] understanding of [her]self" and "trie[s] to undo their acts of refraction," discovering along the way that, in her attempt to "see the way [she] would see in a mirror," she has ended up "paint[ing] an elaborate mural instead" (x, 2019). *Trick Mirror* is an extended contemplation of the impossibility of full self-understanding or self-representation; Tolentino is aware of the convention for contemporary critical writing to start from the self, but wants to resist that disclosure at the same time. What I read, and identify with, in her book is an impulse to think about personal experience as both significant and opaque. I long to break down the walls between theoretical thinking and personal experience, and I also don't want anyone to think that hearing or reading details about my personal life means that they know me. I don't much mind being related to, but I don't want to have to cannibalize myself in the process.

The imperative toward relatability (and, often, resistance to that imperative) is something of a leitmotif for a generation of writers who came up simmering in the stew of the Internet. This link between relatability and digital self-expression is summed up in Rebecca Mead's 2014 *New Yorker* article "The Scourge of 'Relatability,'" in which she describes the expectation of relatability as a twenty-first century phenomenon, one that began with the aesthetics of daytime television but has since expanded into film, literature, even fashion. But what does relatability mean, and how is it distinct from the more general (and much older) desire to identify with characters in works of art? Mead explains:

[T]o demand that a work be "relatable" expresses a different expectation: that the work itself be somehow accommodating to, or reflective of, the experience of the reader or viewer. The reader or viewer remains passive in the face of the book or movie or play: she expects the work to be done for her. If the concept of identification suggested that an individual experiences a work as a mirror in which he might recognize himself, the notion of relatability implies that the work in question serves like a selfie: a flattering confirmation of an individual's solipsism. (2014)

This definition doesn't quite hold up to her examples. So many things are labelled relatable that it's hard to imagine were created for the purpose of accommodating viewers' solipsistic desires, such as a designer's clothes having "relatable shapes." But Mead's central point is clear: lazy reading and viewing habits are producing worse art, art that doesn't challenge us but panders to our desires for uncomplicated, self-affirming, selfie-like representations. The question the article doesn't address is exactly who this "we" might be; if art is meant to reflect us, it must have an *us* in mind.

The answer to that question comes from the examples Mead provides. Despite the article opening with an anecdote about podcaster Ira Glass rejecting Shakespeare for being inadequately relatable, the culture that reproduces relatability—daytime and reality television, YA novels, the show *Girls*, and of course self-ies—alongside the photograph that accompanies the article, all point to a presumed audience of white women. The description of relatability as being akin to selfies particularly adds a gendered dimension to Mead's mistrust of the Internet's all-confession-all-the-time ethos. Selfies are, after all, their own form of digital life-writing, a genre as complex and multi-faceted as any other kind of self-portraiture, and just as deeply embedded in complex histories and discourses: feminine vanity, the objectification of women's bodies, feminist reclamation of our right to represent ourselves, and so on. Alexandra Georgakopoulou calls selfies "small stories," a form of narrative characterized by fragmenta-tion, open-endedness and ongoingness, as well as "a tendency for reporting mundane, ordinary and, in some cases, trivial events from the poster's everyday life" (2016, 302). Rather than seeing selfies as narcissistic, Georgakopoulou argues that we should read them as "contextualized and co-constructed pres-entations of self, shaped by media affordances" (301). Another way of thinking about relatable narratives is to see them as mun-dane, ordinary, and trivial—as imbuing with narrative worth the kinds of events and experiences that often don't appear in more culturally valued stories. Are these ordinary stories the opposite of heroism? Is relatability something like a twenty-first century digitally mediated articulation of sentimentality, with its atten-tion to the smallness and interiority of women's lives?

As with sentimentality, hasty rejections of relatability always feel a touch misogynistic to me, even while I recognize the way that relatability as a broad demand of art is reductive at best, and at worst, a deadening of our collective capacity for empathy. I worry that the rejection of certain aesthetics and reading practices becomes an excuse not to spend more time thinking about how they work and why they are popular. As scholar June Howard writes of sentimentality, the role of the critic is not to decide once and for all "whether the form is complicit with or subversive of dominant ideology" (1999, 64), but to ask, again and again, what work is this art doing? Who is it for, and who is it excluding, and why? Different forms of cultural production ask different questions of us, and as a critic I find myself drawn to certain questions over others. But reading the right kinds of texts in the right kinds of ways, to recall my earlier discussion of anti-racist reading lists, is not a stand-in for ethics or politics. Writing a list of art that deserves to be rejected because it hinges on notions of familiarity or comfort is no better a starting point for understanding how culture works than writing down a list of important books that will make white people less racist just by reading them—or, as I've already argued, by expressing the mere intention to read them. The expectations we place on art—that it should make us more empathetic, for example—can, in fact, be deeply depoliticizing when we treat art as an end in itself, rather than a place to begin from. If the value of reading lies in collective grappling with meaning-making, then the rise of relatable art invites another experience of meaning-making via the art itself, and the kinds of conversations being collectively developed from it. The same goes for sentimental art, which has been critically rejected for reasons so similar to the rejection of relatability that it's hard *not* to read them as, well, related.

---

Sentimentality and relatability are both normative and conventional, based on the idea of a shared emotional experience that they are also actively producing through the *re*production of cultural conventions the audience is assumed to identify with. Lauren Berlant describes the community generated by these shared emotions and identities as the intimate public sphere; the sentimental texts that circulate in these intimate publics interpellate the consumers into a shared world view based on "a broadly common historical experience" that may or may not match up with their actual lived experiences (2008, viii). Intimate publics organized around mass culture are also markets. They give us insight into how capitalist culture has successfully marketed conventionality as a solution for the very problems that capitalism itself is creating: the legal, economic, and social conditions that stand in the way of actual human flourishing (Berlant 2008, 31). The clearest example, for me, is romance novels; as a romance reader, I find the narratives effective not despite, but because of, their normativity. I know what kinds of desires (heterosexual romance, biological reproduction, domestic and financial security, and so on) are being invoked, and I can experience the intimate pleasures of these norms, despite the fact that I don't actually *want* any of them. What I *do* want, though, is the satisfaction of the emotional experiences that romance novels reproduce; I want to be cared for and sheltered from the violence of the world. The desires of the intimate public sphere are the desires to be safe, to be protected from the winds of world-historical events, and on another level, the desire to want those very things offered— and to discard intimate desires, queer and feminist desires, that do not fit. Romance publishing, as an industry, very successfully markets those normative desires to millions of readers.

The problem with sentimentality and relatability is not inherent in how they invite us into community around shared emotional experiences, however. The problem is how they sell us conventionality and call it politics. Feeling seen by a text that describes your own intimate experiences can be a starting point, but naming something as relatable can also be a dead end. Let me illustrate this with an example. In December 2017, *The New Yorker* published a short story that went unexpectedly viral. "Cat Person," by Kristen Roupenian, is the story of twenty-year-old college student, Margot, and her brief relationship with an older man named Robert. Narrated in the third person, the story is told from Margot's perspective, keeping readers close to her internal world as it unfurls a toxic relationship, and using that proximity to hold them in the present of the relationship's unfolding. Readers see how carefully Margot observes and documents Robert's behaviour, modulating her own actions to please him, worrying almost obsessively over whether he's upset with her. They also see how Margot's interpretation of Robert's behaviour is deeply self-involved, tied up in fantasies of her own emotional and sexual value. She's proud of herself for her ability to read him; it makes her feel "powerful, because once she knew how to hurt him she also knew how he could be soothed" (Roupenian 2017). During their single awkward sexual encounter, she finds her own desire stoked by picturing herself through his eyes, a scene that evokes how young women who grew up online learned to see ourselves refracted through the gazes of others as well as our own self-representations. The story speaks to the power and danger of the fantastical intimate life, in which we become real to ourselves insofar as we can imagine ourselves into being the right kind of women who want the right kinds of things.

But what made "Cat Person" a real viral sensation was the way it incorporated the banality of sexual and gendered violence into the smallness of a date gone wrong. As Robert drives Margot home, she thinks, "Maybe he'll murder me now" (2017). The final lines of the story, when Robert's attention seamlessly transitions into harassment, reaffirms the latent possibility of violence women experience in all interactions with men, reframing Margot's obsessive attention to Robert's moods not as a manipulative desire to make him like her, but as a survival strategy. To many readers, "Cat Person" felt like an iconic narrative for the #MeToo moment, one that dramatized the kinds of gendered microaggressions that so many women have experienced but didn't know we were allowed to name as violence. On Twitter, women shared the story enthusiastically, praising it for its fidelity to a very specific set of experiences, experiences so banal that they are rarely represented in art. Over and over again, the story was posted by mostly white women who described it as "brutally and uncomfortably relatable," "brilliantly/depressingly relatable," "uncanny valley levels of relatable," "horrifyingly relatable." This was not the "it's me I'm that" register in which people respond to memes of fat cats (#chomnk), but an example of Berlant's intimate public as a space in which self-recognition through texts—whether or not they represent experiences we have actually had—is valued as an affirmation of the reality of our lives (2008). "Cat Person" was useful, in that moment, because it became the text that allowed women to articulate a particular kind of complaint. It was also useful to *The New Yorker* because the story's virality financially benefited the magazine, and useful to Roupenian herself, who got a book and a movie deal out of it. The capacity for Margot's story to stand-in as a representation of a collective experience had both emotional and financial value—and it served as a reminder of whose experiences can be circulated and marketed as relatable.

The production of relatability within mass-market women's culture is rooted in whiteness: the idea that white women's experiences in particular are universalizable is central to the idea of a women's culture founded on what Berlant calls "a certain emotional generality among women" (2008, 6). It is no accident that the experiences and feelings made to represent this "generality" are experienced and felt by thin, non-disabled, straight white women. As Rebecca Liu explains in the excellent "The Making of a Millennial Woman," artists and cultural producers like Roupenian as well as Lena Dunham, Sally Rooney, and Phoebe Waller-Bridge don't "enjoy full command of the neutral I," inflected as they are by gender, but their whiteness nonetheless positions them as, if not fully universal, then most definitely relatable. And relatability, Liu explains, "leads only to dead ends, endlessly wielding a 'we' without asking who 'we' really are, or why 'we' are drawn to some stories more than others" (2019). Relatability, like sentimentality, endlessly centres whiteness, and perhaps cannot do otherwise.

In the twenty-first century, relatability has become not just a frequently identified quality of, but almost a requirement for, white women's art—and, by extension, the art of women of colour who seek to break into cultural industries by reproducing the normative, generic expectations of white culture. In "Comping White," Laura McGrath uses the American book publishing industry as a model to explain how cultural industries are built around the presumed universality of white authors' work, and thus demand that writers of colour produce work that can be sold via its comparison to popular white art. Comps, or comparative titles, drive publishers' acquisition decisions, including what kinds of advances they offer authors, how many copies of a title they print, and what kind of marketing budget they invest in a given work. Despite the increasing visibility of books by people of colour on literary award shortlists and course syllabi, McGrath demonstrates that the publishing industry continues to centre whiteness by disproportionately using books by white authors as comp titles. Authors like N.K. Jemisin and Celeste Ng—rare examples of authors of colour whose books are used as comps—had to prove themselves through unparalleled levels of commercial and critical success, while white authors can "churn out book after book in a trendy series" (McGrath 2019). It will be a sign of equity in the cultural industries when creators of colour are not only celebrated for their remarkable successes, but also allowed to be less than brilliant, maybe just okay.

The entanglement of relatability with white femininity helps to explain why white women continue to dominate certain sectors of publishing and cultural production in general; when excellence is a precondition of women of colour being recognized as significant artists, that precludes them from being "just like us." Insofar as relatable and sentimental art works to produce an intimate public sphere of white women's presumed shared feelings, it's hard to imagine how they can serve as the ground for feminist world-building, which demands a decentring of white femininity. But the act of creating real or imagined communities around shared texts, emotions, and experiences does not belong to capitalism or to whiteness. I had the opportunity to hear Berlant speak not long before their death in June 2021.[3] Their talk, entitled "The Unfinished Business of Cruel Optimism," explored intimate publics as a site of potential—not throwing aside their well-documented critique of how depoliticizing they can be, but rather attending to what they might make possible. We turn to intimate publics in moments of crisis, sometimes united only by the recognition that something is wrong. And while those publics can be used to sell us a fantasy of comfort and safety and normativity, they also offer a potential space for connection beyond these fantasies. Organized around an affective commitment to a shared set of concerns, intimate publics are about showing up for one another. They might come and go, Berlant argued, but they can be a starting point for collective action, for building something together.

Because intimate public spheres activate shared vocabularies of emotion and experience, they often circulate through the banal repetition of shared genres. Romance novels, with their comfortably familiar tropes and guaranteed happy endings, are certainly an example, but so are selfies, Facebook updates, and confessional blog posts. Digital life-writing has profoundly shaped contemporary literature and the cultural industries, in good and bad ways. On the one hand, the personal essay boom has created a cultural landscape in which writers often feel obliged to draw out their personal traumas for clicks. As *Slate* editorial director Laura Bennett explains in "The First-Person Industrial Complex," the Internet apparently has a "bottomless appetite for harrowing personal essays" (2015). As more and more of these essays are written, the bar for shocking jaded Internet readers is set ever higher, and the people who profit off this hyper-confessional writing are rarely, if ever, the writers themselves. But personal essays also owe much of their DNA to blogging, with its impulse to draw together new forms of online communities around the sharing of often underrepresented perspectives.

When I took to Twitter, and later to podcasting, to articulate a different kind of academic self, I didn't recognize this larger publishing context. But I did recognize that I was working against the years of academic professionalization that had taught me to place a wall between my ideas and my feelings. I was not trying to be relatable by reasserting myself, my feminist politics and activism. But by virtue of slowly building communities around a shared vocabulary of emotions and experiences, I was in fact participating in an intimate public. Every time I shared something, and someone responded with some version of "me too, I feel that too," I caught a glimpse of the world-building potential of relatability. It has not always been a comfortable experience. Those of us who witnessed the rise of a culture of digital self-disclosure often have a fraught relationship to it—particularly the expectations of oversharing and internal consistency. Part of being relatable, after all, is being fully legible on the terms of the intimate public sphere, a legibility that comes from expressing recognizable fears and desires. The result is that strangers often think they know me, and that coworkers mistake a tweet or podcast episode for an unmediated revelation of my deepest self. When people treat me as though I'm transparent, it can make me feel downright invisible.

---

While many creators are actively trading in, and attempting to profit off, their own relatability, others who came up in the same era—of blogging and social media's cultivation of the commercial online self—have begun to produce work that subverts the conventions of digital life-writing. Writers like Daniel M. Lavery, Carmen Maria Machado, and Aminatou Sow and Ann Friedman—all, notably, millennials of the same generation as Tolentino, Roupenian, and myself—have recently published books that play with sentimental norms. Sow and Friedman, for example, published *Big Friendship* in 2020, a book that tells the story of their friendship made famous by their successful podcast *Call Your Girlfriend*. In the book, Sow and Friedman grapple with the realities of a relationship that is at once intimate and public, a real friendship and a performance of friendship that comes loaded with listener expectations and financial implications. As the podcast has become an increasingly central source of income for them both, the navigation of their relationship has become correspondingly more complex.

What's striking about this friendship memoir is how it exposes the seams in the public performance of friendship and identity, pointing to how, as their popular podcast gained momentum and they became representatives of the very idea of twenty-first century female friendship, their personal relationship was falling apart. They acknowledge these seams explicitly in the introduction: "If you listen to our podcast, you are probably screaming right now...because our show is premised on us being tight-knit besties. (Stay sexy and don't fake your friendship to keep your podcast afloat!) You might feel like we played you" (Sow and Friedman 2020, xvi). The ironic reference to the tagline of popular true crime podcast *My Favorite Murder* ("stay sexy and don't get murdered") points to the complexity of friendship-as-brand. *Big Friendship* has a happy ending—it would have to, being a co-written and co-promoted book—but its interrogation of the performance of friendship subtly weaves through the book as a whole, reminding readers of the irreconcilable gulf between the lives performed for us through digital life-writing (including podcasts), and the experiences that don't make the cut.

Other recent memoirs push even further into the resistance of self-disclosure and the expectations of relatability. Lavery's *Something That May Shock and Discredit You*—his third book, but the first to deal explicitly with his transition—opens with an essay that asserts its own deep specificity by playfully invoking and then refuting the possibilities of identification. In "When You Were Younger and You Got Home Early and You Were the First one Home and No One Else Was Out on the Street, Did You Ever Worry That the Rapture Had Happened without You? I Did," the extended call-and-response structure of the title suggests that Lavery is asking the reader to relate. But the deep specificity of the moment that readers are being asked to relate to, along with the immediately inserted "I did," also function as assertions of difference. As the essay continues, he weaves together a child's understanding of Christian rapture theology with the experience of transition as a "sudden shift in self-awareness" (Lavery 2020, 3). Framed by the second-person address of the title, this experience evokes early novelistic conventions (Lavery has spoken of his indebtedness to *Pilgrim's Progress*, for example), inviting readers into an experience of identification as well as transformation by linking conversion narratives to transition narratives. In its final lines, the essay returns to the second person, once again inviting readers into a sense of shared disclosure: "If you don't squeeze through the door at first, just wait patiently for Heaven to grind you into a shape that fits" (2020, 6). Surely we have all experienced something like this grinding.

This tension between disclosure and refusal ramps up in the essay that follows, the first of many pieces in the book identified as "interludes," this one "Chapter Titles from the On the Nose, Po-Faced Transmasculine Memoir I Am Trying Not to Write." The opening paragraph of this interlude directs the reader's attention to the generic expectations of the memoir, particularly the memoir of transition, and in so doing promises that this book will operate differently:

> I am tempted always to make some force or organization outside of myself responsible for my own discomfort, to retroactively apply consistency to my sense of self as a child, to wax poetic about something in order to cover up uncertainty, to overshare in great detail out of fear that the details will be dragged out of me if I don't volunteer them first, and to lapse into cliché in order to get what I want as quickly as possible. (Lavery 2020, 7)

This description of memoir-writing as a series of artistic sleights of hand that obfuscate to create the illusion of transparency sets the reader up for the book that is actually about to follow, one that is in part about Lavery's transition, yes, but never straight-on, always refracted. These refractions draw on the bevy of historical and mythological figures that Lavery made a name for himself writing about on the feminist humour site he co-founded with Nicole Cliffe, *The Toast*. One of the great pleasures of *The Toast* was its esoteric hodgepodge of personal essays, jokes about art history, poetry parodies, advice columns, and videos of Lavery doing impressions of Joan Didion and Anna Wintour. The site captured some of the appeal of other feminist blogs like *Jezebel*, with their combination of personal essays, pop culture, and political commentary, but added a distinctive weirdness that appealed both to the bookish and meme-loving crowds. It's hard to imagine another place where a recurring feature like "Misandrist Lullabies" would fit alongside serious advice about how to buy a car (without interacting with a human). Like *The Toast, Something That May Shock and Discredit You* brings together postmodern pastiche with premodern novelistic conventions, harkening back to a time before art was treated as a window into the artist's true self. Instead, in the tradition of John Bunyan and Daniel Defoe, Lavery refuses the stable signifier of a confessional "I," constantly refracting his authorial self through Apollo and Hyacinthus, Lord Byron, Marcus Aurelius, Jacob wrestling the Angel, Columbo, Sir Gawain, and more. The seeming invitation into close identification with the author, and into the accompanying experience of learning and changing through reading is raised, only to be refused.

A different kind of refracting and refusal is at work in Carmen Maria Machado's *In the Dream House*, a memoir about an abusive relationship and the impossibility of representing the realities of abuse and trauma. While the memoir opens in the first person—it begins with the claim "I never read prologues" (2019, 3)—it quickly switches to a second-person voice that externalizes the experiences being recounted: "I thought you died, but writing this, I'm not sure you did" (14). The grammatical gap between the "I" of Machado's authorial voice and the "you" experiencing the traumatic events being recounted again refuses the transparency and intimacy expected from memoir, a refusal that is further complicated by the text's form. It is written in a series of fragments, each titled "Dream House as" followed by a genre, place, or trope: Dream House as Queer Villainy, Lesbian Pulp Novel, Chekhov's Gun, Unreliable Narrator, Parallel Universe, and so on. The memoir thus explores the unrepresentability of trauma by attempting to represent it again and again, in a hundred different ways, each attempt providing only a glimpse, and exposing the inability of any one glimpse to encompass the whole experience. This genre play also lets Machado represent another unrepresentable story: that of queer domestic abuse. Our narratives of abuse circle around the image of the sentimental heroine, a straight white woman who is vulnerable to the violence of men, particularly violence done in domestic spaces. In "Dream House as Comedy of Errors," Machado describes how difficult it is to find narratives of abuse in queer relationships: "Our culture does not have an investment in helping queer folks understand what their experiences *mean*" (2019, 139).

As with Lavery's memoir in essays and interludes, *In the Dream House* proceeds through metaphor, analogy, and constant shifting deferral because the topic itself is too unnamable, too uncanny. "Putting language to something for which you have no language is no easy feat," Machado explains in "Dream House as Naming the Animals" (134). And, like Lavery's memoir, *In the Dream House* is a decidedly queer take on the genre, one that embraces the liminality and unrepresentability of queerness itself, proceeding not through the bald-facedness of narrative but through metatextual sleights of hand and lateral moves. Machado quotes queer theorist José Esteban Muñoz: "The key to queering evidence, and by that I mean the ways in which we prove queerness and read queerness, is by suturing it to the concept of ephemera. Think of ephemera as a trace, the remains, the things that are left, hanging in the air like a rumor" (qtd. in 2019, 225). I underlined this passage when I first read the book, and I've come back to it again and again, caught on the tension between evidence and ephemera, between that which at least claims to tell a story directly and the traces that hint at a story left untold, perhaps untellable.

In the piling up of ephemera, through lists and inventories and traces, I find some kernel of potential—some way to think through relatability not as a tool of capitalism that demands we commodify everything, including ourselves, but rather as an invitation. Attending to the ephemera of our lives, telling one another who we are and what is important to us, is the first stage in building a world together. The books I've discussed aren't a departure from the conventions of sentimental literature or digital life-writing, so much as rich and complex engagements with these conventions. Relatability is the water in which these memoirs swim, and their subversion works through awareness of how relatability structures readerly expectations. These queer, trans, and racialized writers aren't offering up the self for consumption, voyeurism, or a seamless, difference-erasing identification, but are instead taking up and refracting the personal essay. The small, odd, and queer stories in these books remind us that selfies can also be small, odd, and queer stories, that what might at first be dismissed as a normative drive toward flattering solipsism can, in fact, be the opposite.

As I write this, I think of the queer slippages in Louisa May Alcott's books, and of the long history of queer writers working within the dominant genres of their day while also offering glimpses of another world that might be possible. Intimate publics, said Berlant, are about showing up for one another. One version of showing up is reading carefully and attending to the traces of difference and sameness that weave through the stories people tell us about themselves. Another version is trying our hands at telling those stories ourselves. I like social media because I get to tell you what my life is like and hear about yours, and because these small stories, in their open-ended fragmentation and day-to-day triviality, give us a chance to show up for one another in real time. Academia discourages self-disclosure and intimacy, because relatability and expertise are at odds, particularly for women. The more likeable I am, the less seriously I'll be taken, and vice versa. When I chose to articulate myself differently, on different platforms and for different publics, I gave up that expertise and chose another way through.

I chose relatability, I suppose, and for all my ambivalence toward it, I remain attuned to its potential. The conventions of digital self-disclosure may be entangled with the normativity of the intimate public sphere, but they can also be taken up to ask: what if what we want is not the same? What if we are not beginning from a common ground of feelings, fantasies, or desires? What other forms of intimacy and identification might be available to us? What language can we find to tell one another stories about our lives, to pile up ephemeral traces that say I am here, and you are here, and we are here together?

# WORDS WITH FRIENDS

FOR ME, THERE HAS BEEN NO BETTER LESSON IN THE pleasures and risks of digital life-writing than becoming a podcaster.

I started podcasting in 2015, when my friend Marcelle Kosman and I decided to reread the Harry Potter books together and then, belatedly, to record our conversations. We were both at liminal points in our lives then, living in Edmonton, a city we both liked but didn't think we could commit to if we wanted to stay on the job market, thinking forward to the possibilities of academic careers that felt deeply precarious and all the more desirable for their near impossibility. I remember spending that year bracing myself for the very real likelihood that no university would hire me and beginning to ask the hard questions: what do I actually want to do? What kind of life do I want to live? Nowhere was home, then; not Ottawa, which most of my family and close friends had also left; not Guelph or Edmonton or Edinburgh, which had been way stations on a journey to an increasingly uncertain destination.

We recorded the first episode of *Witch, Please* in Marcelle's tiny downtown Edmonton apartment, a bachelor unit with pretensions of being a one bedroom but walls that didn't quite reach its industrial ceilings. I loved that apartment. It was right on the LRT line so I could stay late, get staggeringly drunk, and not worry about getting home. Later Marcelle moved to a house in Old Strathcona with a yard and a huge raspberry patch, which was objectively better for gatherings but further from transit; I can still feel my thighs going numb in the deep cold of a Prairie winter as I speed-walk up to Whyte Ave to catch the bus. We usually recorded at Marcelle's place, because her partner Trevor was our unpaid tech support, helping us to set up the audio recorder, making sure the batteries were charged and that our laughter wasn't spiking the levels. We only had one mic then, which we would pass back and forth, an accidentally feminist method that forced us to give each other space and time to really articulate a thought. When later, at live events, we had our own mics, Marcelle often had to tell me that actually, she was *not done speaking yet*.

In that first episode, we were making things up as we went. We'd both reread *Harry Potter and the Philosopher's Stone* and taken notes about what we wanted to talk about. Sitting on her couch, we started to divide those points into themes, and then into segment ideas: Granger Danger, for our discussions of Hermione Granger and the representation of women in the books; The Forbidden Forest, for how the wizarding world handles race, disability, and other forms of textual othering. All the segment names were Marcelle's idea, as were the sound effects she edited into our first episode, creating the whimsical audio palette that would come to define the show. My job was to keep us on track and make sure what we were saying made sense. We charted a rough outline for ourselves and, toward the bottom of our first bottle of wine that evening, hit record.

I love going back to that first episode and listening to how nervous we sound, how fuzzy the audio is. Marcelle introduces the podcast as a discussion of our "feelings and thoughts" on the Harry Potter world and I think that order is right; *Witch, Please* was always meant to be an experiment in putting feelings back into our reading, even as our feelings about books were being rigorously professionalized out of us. In her 2015 article "When Nothing is Cool," English scholar Lisa Ruddick identifies this problem in the academic study of literature, pointing to the "unaccountable feelings of confusion, inhibition, and loss" that students often feel in grad school as they're taught that the way they've always related to books is wrong, or insufficiently critical (2015). Drawing on what Eve Sedgwick identified as "a strain of 'hatred' in criticism" as well as Bruno Latour's articulation of "how scholars slip from 'critique' into 'critical barbarity,'" Ruddick bemoans the "thrill of destruction" and the ruthlessness and cruelty of much contemporary criticism. "The only way now to replenish academic discourse," she concludes, "is through innumerable tiny acts of courage in which people say the uncool things" (2015). Those uncool things, for her, are primarily about attachments outside of the institution, pleasures and identities that allow us to hold parts of ourselves away from the work of being scholars and critics. "The greedy institution has a stake, altogether, in impoverishing its members' object worlds," Ruddick concludes. "It promotes a hollowness, which can then be compensated with the satisfactions of status and affiliation within the group" (2015). Our objects—Ruddick points toward monogamous romance and religious faith—are always positioned as things we need to interrogate, critique, and dismantle.

I, for one, *love* critiquing my objects. When I saw Lauren Berlant speak, in November 2020, on "The Unfinished Business of Cruel Optimism," I was taken by their argument that scholars are constantly working to transform our objects, by which they meant both our objects of study and our objects of sentimental attachment. It might seem, then, that sentimentality and critique are opposites, that we cannot love something and interrogate it at the same time, but I don't think that division is quite right. Emotional attachments can be a starting point for collective transformation; we show up for one another when we care about the same thing, but what we do with that thing we care about is up to us. The premise that critique and love are at odds has often come up in discussions of the "post-critical turn"—a scholarly movement interested in the role of affective responses in literary criticism—but again, I think that's a bit of a mischaracterization. Toril Moi describes post-critique as a "willingness to look and see, to pay maximal attention to the words on the page" (2017, 179). In this sense, post-critique is more about readerly agency in relation to texts, about the fact that meaning lies not in what a text itself is doing, but rather in what we *as readers* do with it.

Unsurprisingly, post-critique can slide into a sort of academic version of "let people enjoy things," a rallying cry of the pop culture lover. My response to that is cultural critic Kate

Wagner's excellent piece, "Don't Let People Enjoy Things," in which she describes the franchises people are often demanding the right to enjoy uncritically (in this case, Game of Thrones and the Marvel Cinematic Universe) as "multi-billion-dollar corporate entities engineered to entertain in the same way Doritos are made so that you can't eat just one" (2019).[1] We must not uncritically uphold the pleasures of cultural texts at the expense of reckoning with the conditions of their production, and indeed with the violence that our pleasure may be built on. But that doesn't mean rejecting our attachments—it just means thinking about them and being willing to let them go if we realize, as with so many of the normative promises of sentimentality, that they are not serving us.

When I think of scholarship that engages the "uncool" by challenging the conventions of critique, I think of scholar and artist Lucia Lorenzi. In May of 2018, Lucia (I'm going to use her first name here, as I do with Marcelle, because she is my dear friend) began experimenting with using art to respond to the works of Black writers who she didn't get to read as a student, celebrating but also mourning through colour and shape what it meant to engage with texts that matter. On May 9, 2018, she posted a painting to Instagram entitled "Still Tender," after David Chariandy's novel *Soucouyant*. "I used gold and copper paints not only because of how they reflect the light," she explained in the caption, "but also because they speak to a beauty in woundedness, a kind of gilded sorrow" (Lorenzi 2018). Later, in part as a response to the COVID-19 pandemic, she shifted to the more minimalist medium of India ink, creating works that represented her experiences of chronic illness, her responses to the pandemic and the Black Lives Matter protests. One of those paintings went on to become the cover of Xine Yao's book *Disaffected: The Cultural Politics of Feeling in Nineteenth-Century America*. In the acknowledgements to the book, Xine describes the experience of seeing Lucia's painting:

> On April 10, 2020, during the first COVID-19 lockdown, Lucia shared on Instagram the third in her ink painting series "About Touch and Intimacy during the Pandemic." In the caption, she remarked, "Not sure how to resolve the piece yet, so I'm stepping away from it, turning it around, seeing what works so far." A continent and an ocean away, I was mesmerized by her creative rendition of the paradoxes of intimacy and distance that spoke to my work as I struggled to finish it. Thank you, friend, for generously sharing your gorgeous artwork with me. To me, this collaboration of sorts captures something of the queer of color ethos, femme survival, and Black-Asian counterintimacies that informs the feeling otherwises of Disaffected. (2021, xiii–ix)

The possibilities of intimacy and attachment that Lucia's work opens up, alongside the way it evokes responsiveness and collaboration from other femmes of colour, point to a version of critical engagement that isn't about dismantling or clinging to our objects. These works aren't a rallying cry to let people enjoy things without theorizing their enjoyment; they're a recognition that feelings and ideas are not at odds.

When Marcelle and I started making *Witch, Please*, our giggly and half-drunk podcast still felt pretty damned uncool. We cried, we swore, we talked about our bodies and our feelings, and we were unabashedly and unironically invested in a popular literary property—not just the books, but the movies, plays, even theme parks.[2] When, in June of 2020, Harry Potter author J. K. Rowling outed herself as a TERF (a trans-exclusive radical feminist, a term for self-identified feminists who claim that trans women aren't "really" women), social media was full of people triumphantly announcing that they had never liked, or even read, her iconic books, or that the books were silly and anyone betrayed by Rowling's hateful politics was naive, a bad reader. That response wasn't so much a reversal of how people had treated Rowling previously, but the other side of the same coin. The Harry Potter series has frequently been held up as an exemplar of the way that reading can make people more empathetic. When the author of the series began to proudly declare her *lack* of empathy, that equation was reversed: rather than the books making you good, they must make you bad, which meant *not* liking them was, in fact, morally superior. In this contemporary moment, when any beloved creator might suddenly be revealed as abusive, harmful, or bigoted, publicly liking things is a dicey proposition. Better, perhaps, to keep it cool, to position yourself as a little bit better and smarter than your objects of study. For some, that's a safe position to take; it's hard to be hurt from there.[3]

But while critical coolness might feel like safety for some, it is a survival strategy for others, as we do the necessary work of dismantling the dominant narratives that have saturated our cultural landscape. Wresting textual meaning away from the author is often a liberatory act—one need only look at the fan fiction created by queer, trans, racialized, and disabled Harry Potter fans. From the earliest episodes of *Witch, Please*, we have insisted that it is possible to love something and critique it at the same time—that unpacking the problems in a text can produce other pleasures, a truth that many critical fandoms have known for a while.

Nevertheless, having feelings out loud felt like an act of courage at the time. As *Witch, Please* began to pick up steam, and listeners, Marcelle and I were nervous; we felt, instinctively, that public displays of emotions and fandom stripped us of our perceived expertise, that sharing personal details about our lives heightened our vulnerability as young female scholars. Probably the best manifestation of our anxieties happened at a public talk we gave at Nerd Nite Edmonton. Nerd Nite is an event held in cities around the world that invites experts to talk in accessible ways about their area of expertise. When we were invited to talk at Nerd Nite Edmonton, it was an explicit choice on the part of the organizers to include more speakers from humanities disciplines; the event tends to be dominated by STEM fields and, in my anecdotal experience, by a male audience with, at best, an ambivalent relationship to the authority of women speakers. Marcelle and I chose to give a brief introduction to feminist literary criticism, using Harry Potter books as an example. By this point we had a wide enough following that we knew some listeners would be in the audience, but we also had to contend with the Nerd Nite regulars. During the Q&A following our talk, we were quickly taken to task by a physics professor in the audience, who wanted to know two things: first, what's Harry Potter? And second, how old were we?

What distressed me most about this experience was the bone-deep feeling that he was merely putting into words what many others were thinking: that we were unserious scholars, that our attachment to a popular series should embarrass us. Luckily, Marcelle and I are both pretty fundamentally belligerent people, and deeply salty feminists, and a white man mocking us only had the effect of making us double down on our commitment to the work we were doing. We kept making the podcast, kept building our audience, and slowly I began to attend to the other lessons that this foray into podcasting was teaching me. I learned, first and foremost, how hungry people are for an opportunity to participate in critically engaged feminist conversations about cultural texts. I'd internalized the belief that my research interests were too niche and esoteric for most people, but here suddenly were all these strangers asking for advice on reading Michel Foucault for the first time because they agreed that *Discipline and Punish* (1977) seemed like a useful way of understanding Azkaban, the wizarding world's panoptic prison. Lots of our listeners came from outside the university system, and some specifically identified themselves as poor and/or disabled and/or caregivers who had been prevented from attending university because the institution was not designed for them. The more I read about the historical formation of the modern university, the more I realize that these kinds of exclusions are features rather than bugs; if an institution is going to be built on elitism, it needs to be unavailable to some people.

This is probably a glaringly obvious observation, but as a white middle-class woman in a publicly funded post-secondary system, I had believed that access and openness were a shared institutional value. I realized I was wrong when I began to learn about open access publishing, and encountered arguments against it, by academics, that located the value of scholarship and of the university in their exclusiveness. Open access advocate

Martin Paul Eve quotes the most extreme version of this perspective as voiced by Cambridge University Professor of Ancient
History Robin Osborne, who argues that people who want to
read scholarship "must invest in the education prerequisite to
enable them to understand the language used" (qtd. in Eve 2014).
There's a lot going on here (as Eve points out, one of the primary
critiques of Osborne's argument was the existence of humanities
graduates who have this "prerequisite education" but who, upon
graduating, can no longer access said scholarship), but most
glaring for me is this fantasy that the university is the sole site of
knowledge creation, and that we have a right to hoard it away.

I didn't care much about open access publishing until I
realized how transformative scholarly work could be for readers who otherwise weren't able to access it. Frankly, podcasting made me into a real hard-line bitch about open access. I
learned, first-hand, that the world is full of people outside the
university system who are not only smart enough to engage with
scholarship (I mean, *come on*) but who also possess knowledge
and expertise that those of us working in humanities disciplines
should be engaging with. I'm particularly taken by Rebekka
Kiesewetter's recent call to trace an alternative genealogy of
the open access movement via "the activism of (black) feminist, queer, and labour-related grassroots movements" including
the Kitchen Table: Women of Color Press and the newspaper of
the Third World Women's Alliance (2020, 115). This genealogy
of open access invites questions about the hierarchies we create around different knowledges and forms of expertise; it also
demands a more expansive understanding of openness that is
not simply about access, but that also considers accountability
to the communities we are building knowledge with.

The second lesson podcasting has taught me is how hungry people within the university system are for examples of scholarship that puts feelings back into the work. Our listeners understood the feminist intervention of the podcast, perhaps better than we did at first. They understood *Witch, Please* as permission to care in a way that, however tacitly, is often frowned upon in academia. For us and our listeners, the podcast became a place where care could be expressed not implicitly, through critical engagement or careful reading, but in an explicitly feminized and personalized, and thus embarrassing, way. And sure, it made us feel vulnerable, and sure, we were a little worried about the impact on our careers, but we also leaned hard into care and accountability. The lessons I learned, first from *Witch, Please* listeners and later from the community that emerged around my second podcast, *Secret Feminist Agenda*, revealed to me my own unthinking transphobia and ableism, pushed me to engage more fully with anti-racist thinking and organizing, and showed me how much richer my understanding could be when I listened to perspectives not my own. This community also taught me how to speak from and about identities that I had previously held apart from my scholarly work. I learned to name and speak from my experiences as a fat woman; I slowly came to understand my asexuality, prompted by listeners' readings of characters like Luna Lovegood and even Voldemort. Making *Witch, Please* taught me about the kind of publicly engaged scholar I wanted to be, not an unassailable talking-head expert but always working in collaboration with, and learning from, my community.

What felt truly transformative about making *Witch, Please* wasn't just the act of passing a microphone back and forth, but the sense that our conversations led toward understandings that belonged to neither one of us, but were created within the time and space of the episode, and expanded via our listeners' responses. Before I became someone who mostly worked with co-creators, I did a lot of research on authorship and collaboration. Attention to collaborative authorship offers a point of feminist intervention into a deeply patriarchal and capitalist construct: the author as genius, as lone creator. Collaboration isn't only discouraged; it's actively erased, in favour of false narratives of artistic and intellectual work that deliberately elide the presence of collaborators. There are some famous examples, like Ezra Pound's near-rewrite of T.S. Eliot's *The Waste Land,* or editor Max Perkins's nigh-authorial editorial interventions in F. Scott Fitzgerald's *The Great Gatsby,* but those examples are well-known because they practically enhance the reputation of these brilliant men by adding into the narrative other, also brilliant, also white, also men. We hear less about Vivienne Haigh-Wood's interventions in *The Waste Land,* or F. Scott's theft of material from Zelda Fitzgerald's diary, and we hear nothing at all about generations of wives, daughters, mothers, sisters, and domestic workers who were pulled, willingly or otherwise, into the work of co-creation, and whose contributions weren't even erased because they were never acknowledged to begin with. Authorship as a concept wasn't invented for them.

Collaboration can feel dangerous for women, because it has been wielded against us, to silence us. But collaboration can also allow for forms of co-creation that are embedded in the radical possibilities of feminist friendship. *Witch, Please* brought me joy from the beginning. I didn't realize how important it would be until later, when people started telling Marcelle and me what it meant to them. But that joy and importance were both arrived at collectively. The joy of collaborating with Marcelle is very simple: I think that she's brilliant, funny, and insightful, and talking to her about ideas brings me great pleasure, because she is my friend and I love her. We arrived quickly at a rhythm of conversation and collaborative thinking that gained energy not through critiquing each other but by building on each other's ideas. "Yes," we'd say, "yes, absolutely, and that makes me think of this." I don't think it's a coincidence that listeners continue to wildly misattribute ideas and jokes to the other person; sure, people aren't very good at telling women's voices apart, but also, our points so often felt shared. I have no desire to take ownership over anything we said on the podcast. (Marcelle might feel differently about that; she loves to get credit for a good joke.) The collective part came later, as the podcast moved through the world and people started to find it and find something in it. Certainly, part of what they found was an opportunity to talk about Harry Potter, to reframe a favourite text through a political lens that many listeners didn't have when they first started reading the series, and perhaps hadn't realized they could put into conversation with these beloved books. But I also think that they found something many of us are hungry for: a meaningful, and meaningfully accountable, feminist community.

In August of 2020, we rebooted *Witch, Please* through a new partnership with the feminist podcast network Not Sorry. To make the reboot possible, we had to find a way to fund the podcast's production; where we had produced the original run ourselves, we were now too busy and needed help. Like many podcasters, we turned to Patreon, an online crowd-funding platform that allows creators to develop sustainable financial support through monthly contributions from members interested in their work. To run a successful Patreon campaign, you need bonuses—special content that members can unlock by supporting the project at different financial levels. We decided to make our basic bonus content something that listeners had been requesting for years: access to the unedited recordings of the podcast's original run.

Our listeners' desire for these unedited episodes has the same origin as Patreon itself: the heightened capacity for podcasting in particular, and digital forms of life-writing in general, to produce a sense of intimacy between strangers, an emotional connection mediated by these new, born-digital forms of sentimental narratives. And so, every month, Marcelle and I take turns listening to the unedited conversations we recorded over five years ago, making notes along the way. Each unedited episode is posted with an accompanying content warning—a list of potentially upsetting, triggering, or otherwise difficult things we say—because in that original run, we used language we would not use now. We talked about intelligence in ableist ways, we discussed gender through a cis-normative lens, and we generally assumed a listenership with identities and experiences similar to our own.

But the reason why we wouldn't and don't use that language today is because our listeners did *not* have the same identities and experiences as us, and when we fucked up they definitely told us, and we would apologize, sometimes going back and re-editing previous episodes but mostly committing to keep listening, learning, and doing better. It hasn't always been easy. The process of being called out, whether gently or not, can feel awful. As Marcelle once said, "you're going to screw up and it really sucks, but you won't die from shame and if you're never willing to hear how you can do better, you'll never do better."[4] This collective commitment to trying, together, offers a glimmer of possibility for what intimate feminist publics can be: getting it wrong but continuing to try is one version of showing up. When we decided to release the original audio without substantive changes, it wasn't because we felt great about everything we had said—it was because we didn't want to erase the way our understanding has shifted as a direct result of a community of engaged listeners, thinking alongside and challenging us. We are committed to thinking, and learning, in public.

When I launched my second podcast, *Secret Feminist Agenda*, I was driven by this understanding of the power of podcasting to build community through embodied knowledge and productive difference, rather than normative ideas of shared identity. The temporary nature of my time in Edmonton had shifted to a new form of uncertainty: I had relocated to Vancouver, a city where I knew almost no one, for a permanent faculty position. It was daunting to begin building a new community from scratch in my thirties as a single and childless woman, and I was crushingly lonely, though ashamed to admit it. I had been working toward the goal of securing a tenure-track job for over a decade, so why wasn't I happier? Much like *Witch, Please*, *Secret Feminist Agenda* was a friendship project, but this time the goal was to make new friends. Over the next three years I built a community hand-in-hand with creating the podcast, making friends with guests and making guests of friends. As the show changed, so did I. I had my first experiences of online attacks, and my first brushes with the legal protections that academic freedom offers; I learned what I believed in, and what I wanted to fight for. I learned to tell a new kind of story about myself, about what kind of person I was and what kind of academic I wanted to be, through the conversations and communities that podcasting opened up for me. And throughout the process I continued to experiment with emotional vulnerability, deliberate intimacy, and setting aside the persona of expertise and authority that I had worked so hard to build up.

Even as *Secret Feminist Agenda* was organized around my ideas of collectivity and collaboration, it also taught me about the limitations of shared identity. Podcasting as an example of the digital sentimental encourages self-disclosure and the formation of intimate publics through a focus on what we have in common, how we are alike. But feminist community-building resists this normativity, instead holding space for irreconcilable differences. When Haudenosaunee writer Alicia Elliott spoke with me, she immediately identified her fraught relationship to feminism, outlining the history of nineteenth-century white feminists like Elizabeth Cady Stanton who appropriated Indigenous cultural practices (*Secret Feminist Agenda*, 2.6). A few episodes later I pondered my own limitations as a white woman, grappling with the recognition that, even in my most intimate relationships, I cannot assume that I understand the experiences of my friends who are Black, Indigenous, or people of colour—indeed, that my desire to hold everything, to empathize with every experience, is an extension of the logic of whiteness and its desire for universality (*Secret Feminist Agenda*, 2.9).

Building intimate feminist publics through podcasting has taught me that my experience is not universal, and has brought me back, again and again, to a central problem of the sentimental: how do we care ferociously for one another without demanding that we become collectively legible to one another? The answer I have come up with so far—an answer that is, by definition, subject to revision—is that we do it slowly, and we do it together. Writing conventional scholarship taught me to make my ideas as impermeable as possible, to anticipate and fend off potential critiques, but podcasting has shown me what's possible when I do my thinking out loud and in community. I have put aside my desire for an unassailable version of expertise, and leaned instead into my attachments and emotional investments, realizing that my scholarship is only as good as the conversations it starts.

# GETTING TO KNOW YOU

**LIKE MANY SCHOLARS, I LEARNED TO THINK IN THE FORMS** and genres of my discipline; in the humanities, that's the 25-page seminar paper that turns into the 10,000-word single-authored article, and the 300-page dissertation that turns into the first monograph. The emphasis is on ever-longer and more sustained arguments built out of a single author's original research. These forms and genres have rules that, as scholars of academic writing like Katja Thieme have pointed out, are often unstated and instead absorbed through our own reading, and encouraged or discouraged through gatekeeping processes like grading, and later, peer review (2017). Our ideas aren't determined by these forms, but neither do they have complete free rein. I experience the constraint of academic writing almost kinaesthetically at this point; I sit down to write at the computer, place my fingers on the keyboard, and begin to produce long lines of academic prose, seven- or eight-line sentences that a friend once joked read as if I've challenged myself to use every preposition.

Academic writing, like many other genres of writing, is structured by a set of expectations that operate at the levels of writer, reader, and publisher, though not necessarily in that order. Scholar-turned-novelist Rachel Malik, in "Horizons of the Publishable," argues for a reversal of how book historians generally think about the relationship between writing and publishing. The idea of publishability precedes writing, she argues, framing the possibilities of what can be written (Malik 2008). When I began, then, to chafe against what felt like the limitations of scholarly communication, of what was publishable in the forms and genres I was used to, it is perhaps not surprising that I was drawn to a totally different publishing ecosystem, one with its own horizons and expectations.

Podcasting feels different in my body—my posture is different, my breathing is different—and in my podcasts I have a different voice, one that is much less buried in the genre expectations of academic writing. It is a voice that feels like it's actually mine. That unfettered feeling isn't quite accurate, though; it's not that podcasting freed my voice, so much as it has allowed me to experiment with new registers and new voices. Switching to a different medium, with different affordances, gave me a space to play with the way I did my work, and reminded me of how deeply I'd internalized many of the conventions of humanities scholarship. Nick Couldry uses the term "mediatisation" to get at how digital storytelling is characterized by "a distinctive 'media logic,' that is consistently channeling narrative in one particular direction" (2008, 48). Similarly, Anna Poletti draws on Sidonie Smith and Julia Watson's idea of "coaxed life narrative" to describe this process as "coaxing" (2011, 73). What these various scholars' work have in common is a focus on how digital storytelling is shaped by media and genre conventions, which in turn shape how we describe, or perform, our own identities.

This link between my instinctive sense of podcasting as transformative and the "coaxing" logics of podcasting's own media conventions became clear to me when my podcast *Secret Feminist Agenda* went through an open peer review process. Anna Poletti participated in the review of the podcast's second season, and she framed her response to the project in terms of her research on "contemporary forms of personal storytelling in a range of media (the field of life-writing studies)," with a particular interest in "non-traditional and non-institutional forms of storytelling" ("Review"). Working from this perspective, Poletti explicitly linked the personal storytelling of *Secret Feminist Agenda* to "what feminist and queer scholar Lauren Berlant calls 'the kinesthetics of form'" in terms of "how genre intersects with the affordances of specific media (its modes of production, circulation and reception)" ("Review"). She prompted me to pay attention to how the podcast was challenging the conventional forms of academic knowledge creation "by utilising the modes of address and storytelling that are the staple of the most successful forms of nonfictional podcasting (such as *This American Life*, and *The Moth*)" (Poletti, "Review"). As liberating as the move to podcasting felt, I had to attend to how this new medium had its own constraints that I was now working within—and its own conventions for shaping what kinds of stories I could tell. These stories were not simply different from my own more conventional scholarship, but actively engaged with the very tropes of sentimentality that I once thought academia would help me escape. The conventions of podcasting include attention to feeling—often amplified by editing and music choices—as well as interest in the anecdotal and mundane dimensions of individuals' lives. Where conventional scholarship had taught me to resist personal disclosure, podcasting seemed to demand it.

To better understand what I instinctively felt about making podcasts, I turned to my favourite tool for helping to make sense of my experiences: theory. The question of how digital storytelling might coax out, or even coerce sentimental narratives is central to Poletti's own scholarship. In her article "Coaxing an Intimate Public," she thinks through how digital storytelling, conceived as a democratizing form of life-writing, seeks to bring affect and empathy back into the political realm, particularly by making space for what is often called the "ordinary" voice (Poletti 2011). In fact, the anecdotal and often banal forms that digital life-writing can take go a long way to inventing the idea of the ordinary person, one whose sheer ordinariness becomes part of the significance of their story. Poletti's thinking prompted me to return to a conversation I had years ago, about the kind of podcast storytelling that seems to have sentimentality woven deep into its fabric. The podcast I'm thinking of is a 2016 episode of *This American Life* titled "Tell Me I'm Fat," which features stories by Lindy West, Elna Baker, and Roxane Gay on their experiences with fatness. I loved this episode when I first listened to it; it resonated with me so powerfully that I thought of sending it to my parents (I didn't; I was still years away from having a frank conversation with them about fatphobia). But shortly afterward, during an interview with writer and fat activist Virgie Tovar, my fondness was challenged. Tovar told me about her discomfort with the episode, and with the "white male voyeurism" of *This American Life* in general. She called it "violence and poverty porn" that lacks a clear "call to action," making it less about political organizing than about the middle-class pleasures of discussing other people's oppression over dinner (McGregor 2017, 147). During that conversation, I made the connection between Tovar's description of *This American Life* and sentimental reading practices that aim to evoke feeling in the reader, ideally in order to teach a moral lesson; I recognized how extractive and voyeuristic those practices often are. Her critique of "Tell Me I'm Fat" resonates with Berlant's issue with intimate publics, in which "vulnerability and suffering can become all jumbled together into a scene of the generally human, and the ethical imperative toward social transformation is replaced by a passive and vaguely civic-minded ideal of compassion" (2008, 41–42). When the mere fact of hearing an ordinary person's story, and feeling some way about it, is conflated with social transformation, we end up with a kind of fetishization of human suffering and sentimental responses to it without any actual shift in the power dynamics that produced that suffering in the first place.

The primary claim to ethical value made by podcasts in the style of *This American Life*—human interest non-fiction storytelling—centres around the idea of *story*. Story is a usefully meaningless word, yet the claim that "everyone has a story" has become so strongly associated with *This American Life* and narrative non-fiction podcasting in general that it's basically a trope at this point. In an early episode of the Netflix

animated series *BoJack Horseman*, twenty-something aspir-
ing writer Diane Nguyen's ringtone, voiced by long-time *This
American Life* host and producer Ira Glass himself, announces
her support of public radio: "I'm Ira Glass. Thank you for being
a sustaining member of public radio. Everyone has a story, and
your phone's story is that it's ringing" (Bob-Waksberg 2014).
The same ubiquitous claim—everyone has a story—is articulated without the accompanying irony by radio producer Dave
Isay in the 2010 collection *Reality Radio*. In "Everyone Around
You Has a Story the World Needs to Hear," Isay describes his
StoryCorps project:

> A lot of people talk about crying when they hear
> StoryCorps stories, and it's not because they're sad. I
> think it's because they're hearing something authentic
> and pure, in a time when it's hard to tell what's real and
> what's an advertisement—it's kind of anti–reality TV.
> Nobody comes to StoryCorps to get rich. Nobody comes
> to get famous. These are everyday people talking about
> lives lived with kindness, courage, decency, and dignity,
> and when you hear that kind of story, it sometimes feels
> like you're walking on holy ground. (2017, 169)

What's striking here is Isay's investment in story as fundamentally unmediated—in fact, as verging on the sacred because
it is the opposite of media, as represented here by reality television. And of course these unmediated stories come from
ordinary people who, we must assume by extension, have not
consumed any media themselves and so aren't performing or
mediating their own identities. My own podcasting experience

has taught me the opposite is true: everyone talks differently when they're talking into a microphone, myself included. It took me ages to develop my podcasting voice, one that feels natural to me but surely isn't, if it took me so long to learn. The first season of *Secret Feminist Agenda* provided another significant learning curve, that of figuring out how to coax my own guests into speaking to me as though I wasn't holding a microphone six inches from their faces. I learned that it was easier to talk to people with some media experience, who had practised explaining themselves for multiple audiences, but who weren't on a media circuit and thus coached to deliver canned responses to questions. My favourite episodes are the ones that create the impression of a casual conversation between two friends, but it turns out that two friends actually having a casual conversation on mic doesn't make for good audio. Sounding "ordinary" takes a lot of work.

The focus on drawing authentic and deeply felt stories out of the small details of people's lives is perhaps the most sentimental thing about podcasting. The conventions of first-person address and gradual, even unintentional, self-disclosure, are so ingrained that even fiction podcasts sometimes centre around the voice of a recurring host who reveals personal details in the process of telling a story; Cecil Palmer, the voice of *Welcome to Night Vale*, also hosts a local radio show, while Jonathan Sims, host of *The Magnus Archives*, is preserving the archives of the institute where he works by making analog audio recordings of them. Both hosts gradually reveal details of their own lives, creating a larger frame narrative that individual episodes fit into; both hosts are also voiced by actors using their names (first name, in Cecil Baldwin's case and full name in Jonathan

Sims's case), heightening the sense of verisimilitude and intimacy with these fictional characters. And this intimacy is even further heightened by the way we listen to podcasts. We carry them around in our ears and on our bodies; they weave into the routines of our daily lives, and the discussions gradually become inseparable from our own thoughts. Sometimes that intimacy may resonate with an in-person relationship (many of the listeners to *Secret Feminist Agenda,* for example, are friends or colleagues), but in many cases it does not; what's significant is that the intimacy feels real.

The publishing practices of podcasting amplify this sense of intimacy. In a world of corporately owned algorithms, podcasts are one of the only digital media forms that we actively curate for ourselves, and thus one of the few where big-time industry money isn't required for a show to become a success. As a result, there's still ample room for amateur podcasters, and for a wider range of vocal performances. The sonic qualities that once signalled podcasting's inferiority to radio have been increasingly embraced as deliberate characteristics of podcast production. Voices on radio are professionalized and sonically compressed, while podcasters will deliberately lean into speaking styles that register as more casual (vocal fry, for example, or not editing out filler words such as "like" and "um") or make production choices that signal informality (allowing episodes to vary in length and format, or leaving in sounds that indicate the podcaster's environment, such as pets or children, for example). These differences in how podcasting mediates the human voice can make it sound less mediated than radio, as though you're listening, as podcasters often put it, to "friends in your ears." And while many of these characteristics of early podcasts were simply side effects of their amateur production contexts, they have begun to solidify into conventions, or even listener expectations. Heck, in *Witch, Please* we insisted that leaving baby sounds in the audio is a feminist intervention into patriarchal conceptions of professionalism. If podcasts sound like ordinary people's voices, that's in part because we've been trained to hear them as such—to associate their characteristics with the aesthetics of ordinariness.

---

I've encountered the critical study of ordinariness, also referred to as the banal or the mundane, from a few angles. For instance, my work on the history of women's periodicals led me to theorize how magazines are mundane on multiple levels, from their seriality to their repetitive and quotidian content. On the pages of a household magazine we find a jumble of forms, both lofty and banal—genre fiction, advice columns, political news, and advertisements—all crowded together. This juxtaposition of registers implies that women's lives and domestic labour are as worthy of attention as a royal wedding, or a new railway being built. It took me some time to realize that I was employing a similar approach in *Secret Feminist Agenda*, drawing on anecdotes from my own life and the lives of my guests to make sense of our conversations. In her peer review, Poletti pointed to the podcast's use of anecdotes and asked me to consider whether I'm "seek[ing] to alter scholarly knowledge by bringing it into the existing genre of the anecdote" or "reworking the anecdote to demonstrate that the genre itself can produce knowledge" ("Review"). Am I making knowledge quotidian and thus more accessible, or demonstrating that the quotidian itself has something to teach us?

In response to these prompts, I made episode 3.29, "Feminist Anecdotes," in which I settle on the latter—that my goal is to demonstrate that the anecdote itself can produce knowledge, and I want to explore what kind of knowledge it can create. *Secret Feminist Agenda* is about the insidious, nefarious, insurgent, and mundane ways we enact our feminism in our daily lives. From its conception, I was interested in using podcasting as a form of digital storytelling to explore both the transformative, world-making possibilities of feminism, and its more mundane dimensions. I was particularly interested in drawing these extremes together to think about the links between our everyday experiences and the radical possibilities of feminist theory and practice. In fact, the marriage of theory and practice—or praxis, as it's often called—is kind of the whole point of the podcast. (And yes, my guests have absolutely made fun of me for saying "praxis" too much.)[1] When I think about my desire to link theory with practice, the mundane with the transformative, I think about my own relationship to feminist theory as a body of texts and knowledge. I know that for many people—students and academics alike—theory is alienating, even exclusionary, layered in jargon that makes it inaccessible and seemingly irrelevant to their daily lives. What use was it for me to understand Judith Butler's concept of gender performativity, or Sara Ahmed's notion of the feminist killjoy? Can those ideas help me to navigate the world?

I'm convinced that they can and do. Where theory was once, for me, a technique for externalizing my feelings to avoid feeling them, it has since become a toolkit that helps me to understand my own position in the world more fully. Reading Butler for the first time equipped me with new tools to understand my navigation of the heteronormative world as a queer woman, introducing me to a world of queer theory that has allowed me to imagine living otherwise by finding pleasures and identities outside of those narrow scripts that my early reading of sentimental narratives presented. Ahmed not only transformed my sense of the role that critique plays in the larger project of living a feminist life, but also dispelled my belief in the myth that it was my job to be pleasant, smiling, and accommodating, to prove the validity of feminism by performing happiness. These are theories that have touched me deeply and prosaically, shifting not only how I grapple with big ideas but also how I live my day-to-day life.

And because theory, for me, offers techniques that help to locate us, it always begins from where we are. This rooting of the theoretical in our respective locations and perspectives is an established premise of feminist theory, and it informs the way I use and teach theory in the classroom. I begin from the anecdote—let's understand Foucault's concept of discipline by looking at this classroom; let's understand intersectionality by returning to the specific legal case Kimberlé Crenshaw was grappling with when she first articulated it—because the anecdote gives us a way in and reminds us, from the beginning, that theory is only as valuable as it is useful for helping us to understand and navigate the world. This is how cultural studies scholar Melissa Gregg understands the role of anecdotes: they "offer a discursive space in which a singular idea can be positioned, offered and demonstrated" (2010, 366). This pedagogical framing of the anecdote resonates for me; the anecdote positions, offers, demonstrates—it teaches. Gregg returns to the pedagogical function of the anecdote when she quotes Meaghan Morris on the roles that cultural critics play: we "work primarily as mediators—we are writers, readers, image producers, teachers—in a socially as well as theoretically obscure zone of values, opinion, belief, ideology and emotion" (qtd. in Gregg 2010, 379). Anecdotes mediate the theoretically obscure, doing what Morris calls the "slow work" of gradually shifting "what people take to be thinkable and doable, desirable and liveable, acceptable and unbearable, in their particular historical circumstances" (Gregg 379). This work is slow because it's iterative; we have to keep imagining new worlds until we imagine them into being.

I often joke that my most useful contribution to the world is helping people feel less gaslit by confirming the reality and legitimacy of their experiences, and providing them with theoretical tools to reframe those experiences; this is my version of the slow work of shifting what we consider unbearable. But the process of making *Secret Feminist Agenda* has also been a gradual shift in what *I* consider unbearable. In the seventh episode of the podcast, I told a story about trying to put an IKEA bed frame together by myself, even though the instructions called for two people: "And you know what? It was a disaster. I needed help" (1.7). Articulating this anecdote out loud became an opportunity both to theorize it and to challenge myself to try something different. Three seasons later, I returned to the topic of asking for help to reflect on what I had learned, and examined the role the podcast had played in that learning:

A really interesting side effect of *Secret Feminist Agenda* as a project for me is that it's helped me to stay accountable to my values because I say them out loud [laughs] and not only say them out loud, but like record them and put them on the Internet and then transcribe them and put them in a place where a ton of other people can hear them and respond to them. And that has turned out to be helpful for me in terms of trying to make those ideals and those values something that I practice. And I mean practice in both the sense of praxis, as in taking a theory and making a sort of practical enacted thing, but also practice like you practice a musical instrument, like try to get more skillful at something by doing it regularly until it comes more naturally. (*Secret Feminist Agenda*, 4.27)

The use of anecdotes grounds my thinking about interdependence and accountability in my own lived experience, and I work to not thoughtlessly expand from the specificity of my experience to universal or normative claims. My anecdotes begin here, where I am, like yours begin there, where you are. It's at the level of the everyday—building an IKEA bedframe, for example—that we can discover both where our experiences overlap and where they meaningfully, structurally differ. When we stay grounded with the mundane and the banal, perhaps we can resist leaping immediately to the universalizing impulses of the sentimental. Maybe we can instead pause over other qualities of the sentimental: its interest in embodied emotional responses, domestic culture, intimate reactions to texts, and the particularity of our selves and our lived experiences of the world (Howard 1999, 77).

I keep coming back to the sentimental for its capacity to refocus our attention onto these banal registers, which are worth paying attention to for both their problems and their potential. As Cree poet and scholar Billy-Ray Belcourt explains in "Settler Structures of Bad Feeling," "built into the thorny mechanics of settler colonialism was the racialized production of bad feeling as of a piece with everyday life" (2018). Settler colonialism itself is deeply banal, in the sense that Hannah Arendt uses the term: an evil that disguises its malevolence in its mundane proceduralism. As the history of sentimentality shows us, the cozy domesticity of white femininity is entangled with the violence of colonialism and white supremacy, a fact that we can only grasp if we pay attention to the domestic and the everyday, and the opportunities they provide to pause and reflect on what makes up the textures of our lives, and why. In *The Practice of Everyday Life*, Michel de Certeau demonstrates how institutional strategies often act upon us at the most banal registers, and at the same time these registers are where we can resist (1998). Art that pays attention to the everyday—often by engaging with mundane forms, like the list or inventory—teaches us to pay attention to how the textures and rhythms of our lives are at once significant and wide-ranging. Attentiveness is vital, lest we be lured by sentimental notions of normalcy. Podcasts, with their interests in small and intimate stories, offer a version of this attention.

When I think of podcasts that have cast my own everyday in a different light, *The Secret History of Canada* comes to mind. Created by Leah-Simone Bowen and Falen Johnson in 2018, the show was quickly picked up by CBC Podcasts after its first season. In each episode, Bowen, a first-generation Barbadian

Canadian, and Johnson, Mohawk and Tuscarora (Bear Clan) from Six Nations Grand River Territory, take a deep dive into a seemingly innocuous aspect of Canadian culture or history from a feminist, decolonial, and anti-racist perspective. Both hosts have a background in theatre, which comes through in their ability to balance warm banter with tight scripting and editing. Their very first episode, "The Secret Life of Banff," unpacks the history behind this familiar tourist destination that has come to function as visual shorthand for Canada as an apparently uninhabited winter playground. The episode I keep coming back to, though, is decidedly more mundane. In "Shout Out to Susan Olivia Poole," a two-minute mini-episode released between full-length episodes, they tell the story of the first Indigenous woman in Canada to receive a patent: "And what did she invent, you ask? Well, she invented something a majority of Canadians have used, but probably don't remember using: the Jolly Jumper!" (Bowen and Falen, 2017). Drawing on a practice she recalled from her Ojibwe relatives, Poole reproduced a method for calming babies using stuff she had around the house: a cloth diaper, a metal spring, and an axe handle. The secret history the hosts uncover in this episode is not one of violence but rather of Indigenous brilliance rooted in a combination of Traditional Knowledge and domestic innovation. It's the detail of the axe handle that really does it for me, though. It arrests me in its specificity, prompting me to wonder what it might mean to have a spare axe handle lying around, teasing me with the promise of domestic familiarity overlaid with difference. I don't know a damned thing about Susan Olivia Poole, other than that she was Ojibwe, had seven children, and had a spare axe handle. Those details have stayed with me, long after the more complex histories of Banff, New Brunswick, or Niagara Falls featured on other episodes. It's a small inventory, but a powerful one: cloth diaper, metal spring, axe handle. The ephemeral traces of a life.

———

I've learned a lot about podcasting since I first gushed to Virgie Tovar about the *This American Life* episode "Tell Me I'm Fat," and I returned to this episode with a new perspective: both as a fat person whose politics have become steadily more radical over the past five years, and as a scholar who has been thinking about how podcasts frame the idea of *story*. More than anything, I wanted to feel my way back through this episode and explore how an awareness of its seams—how it's been put together— shifted my reading. Like most episodes of *This American Life*, it's framed as a series of thematically connected audio stories and interviews. It opens with a conversation between Ira Glass and author Lindy West, who at the time was promoting her memoir *Shrill: Notes from a Loud Woman*. West explains why she insists on using the word "fat" to describe herself, while Glass expresses surprise and even discomfort with hearing the word used. After further conversation with West while Glass maintains the same tone—a kind of gentle wonder at what she's describing—the episode moves on to Act Two, a first-person story reported by *This American Life* staffer Elna Baker. In it, Baker tells the story of her own weight loss, achieved by the use of the amphetamine-like diet drug phentermine, and her shock at how differently the world treated her afterward. She describes in graphic detail the pain and humiliation of skin removal surgeries, her horrified realization that her husband of only a month would not have loved the version of herself she calls "old Elna," and the final revelation that she continues to take phentermine: "I am on speed, because I need to stay thin. I need to stay thin so I can get what I want" (*This American Life*, 589). The subsequent pieces—an interview with Roxane Gay about her personal rejection of body positivity discourse, another reported story about the rise of the Christian weight loss movement, and an excerpt from *Shrill*—continue to unfold the curious premise of the entire episode: that fat people ought to be allowed to have rich and fulfilling lives.

At a very basic level, it sucked relistening to this episode. I put it on and went for a long walk, and as I listened, I tried to remember what had felt so good about it the first time around. As much as I love Lindy West's work, it was Elna Baker's story that really struck me on the first listen, her frank confession of what she had put her body through and why; the recognition, implicit in her experiences, that this violent transformation had been driven not by any true desire for thinness but by a kind of grim awareness of what the world demanded of her. Surely anyone hearing this story, I thought, would draw the same conclusion I did: that weight loss was absolutely not worth this suffering, that it was the world that needed to change, not individual women's bodies. But on relistening, I couldn't hear that hope anymore. What I heard was the way each of these women was asked to trot out her body, her pain, and parade it around for a bemused host and an audience of people who presumably had to be convinced to see fat women as fully human. Even Baker's more structural critique of how fatphobia constrains and warps women's lives is lost in the way it's edited together

with the stories of women who are presented as making different choices—as though "choice" is the relevant framing device
in a story about fatphobia. As I listened, I heard the way access
to their pain was the hinge Glass's wonder turned upon, how
the show framed their stories as opportunities to learn from
their experiences, and how that learning was contingent upon
reading their stories as the truth of fat experience, rather than
the kinds of narratives demanded of fat or formerly fat women
if they want to be seen as worthy of care.

In Glass's voice-over he is a neutral observer, not himself a
fat person but a person fat people have been talking to, so now
he understands where they are coming from. His double role
as observer and audience surrogate allows him to teach the
audience how to respond to what they're hearing through his
own modelling—itself another form of coaxing. It's clear the
intended audience is also not fat people, or at least not other
people who are comfortable with being fat, because of how he
frames the conversation: "That's how radical this is. It's saying
that no weight is better than any other weight, which, given the
health risks associated with greater weight that Lindy acknowledges, it can be hard to get your head around" (*This American
Life*, 589). Glass's tone is one of largely benign interest, curious
about West's perspective and those of "people who definitely
do not feel the same way Lindy does about all this"; it's certainly not the voice of someone implicated in the fatphobic
culture the episode will unpack. In fact, Glass implicitly makes
space for the mockery of fat people through segues like "Grab a
Twinkie and come back in a minute." The episode needs Glass's
voice to mediate the irreconcilability of the women's narratives and give them meaning. And therein lies the fundamental

paradox of story as "something authentic and pure," as Isay puts it. Despite being imagined as the opposite of mass cultural mediation, story has to be mediated to make sense. We are always working within genres, cultural contexts, and shared vocabularies of meaning; the right kinds of stories need to be coaxed into being, and someone needs to decide what those right stories are in the first place.

That means that the decision to treat these fat women's stories as curiosities to be offered up to an audience, perhaps as an opportunity to practice their own empathy by seeing a fat woman as human, is a deliberate one, part of a set of choices made at the levels of interviewing, writing, and producing this episode. It also means that we can make different choices about how we tell stories. *Secret Feminist Agenda*, coming on the heels of *Witch, Please,* was an opportunity to further develop my understanding of feminist conversation as a method. I had learned that I loved building ideas together, in real time; I love the rush of a conversation where two people can't get ideas out fast enough, not one-upping each other but weaving thoughts together until they become more than the sum of their parts. One conversation that stands out for its sheer and unexpected enthusiasm was in episode 4.4 of *Secret Feminist Agenda*, with Khairani Barokka. I met "Okka" the same way I meet many of my favourite guests: she had been listening to the podcast, was coming to Vancouver, and so pitched herself for an interview. We met as strangers and talked in my office for two hours: it was incandescent, full of joy, laughter, rage, and the excitement of just encountering each other's minds. I would quote from the transcript here, but it doesn't capture the feeling. I call that feeling *emergence*—an unpredictable complexity that results from the interaction of different components in a complex system. The best classroom conversations are like this as well.

To foster space for emergence in my conversations, though—on podcasts or in classrooms—I've found I need to begin without a clear sense of how the conversation will unfold or conclude. I've almost never written interview questions, and when the conversation is going well, I don't need them (when it's floundering, though, I really regret not having them). The unpredictability of an emergent conversation hinges on the possibility of failure. I can't have an emergent conversation if I'm worried about sounding silly or letting go of my expertise. I have to be ready for the whole thing to fall apart. That unpredictability, though, doesn't mean that emergence is a natural or spontaneous quality; it's as coaxed as the so-called ordinary stories we hear on *This American Life.* Part of the learning curve of making *Secret Feminist Agenda* was figuring out how to coax my guests into that kind of openness. At the beginning of my episode with Okka, she was surprised to discover that I was already recording. I mentioned that Ames Hawkins (who I had talked to in episode 3.26) suggested I might want to tutor guests, to prepare them for the kind of conversation to come. I joked to Okka that I had ignored Ames—"I was like, nah. They're gonna figure it out. It'll be fine"—but in actual fact, Ames had reminded me that naturalness is not all that natural. No form of storytelling is.

This paradox lies at the heart of Jessica Abel's 2015 graphic narrative-cum-guidebook *Out on the Wire: The Storytelling Secrets of the New Masters of Radio.* The book, which is described as "uncover[ing] just how radio producers construct narrative," glosses storytelling radio as a form that uses "personal stories to breathe life into complex ideas and issues" to "help us to understand ourselves and our world a little bit better" (Abel 2015, back copy). What's distinct about how radio and podcasting intertwine the individual with the universal is the use of voice as a way of embedding larger issues in the intimate perspectives of specific speakers. The foreword by Ira Glass emphasizes the ever-increasing popularity of storytelling radio and podcasts—pointing to NPR's *Invisibilia* gaining "over two million listeners per episode in four weeks" and each episode of *Serial* being downloaded by over seven million people—before going on to invite the reader to join the world of storytellers (qtd. in Abel 2015, ix). What follows is an account of just how these storytelling experts (including Jad Abumrad and Robert Krulwich, Alex Blumberg, Glynn Washington, and Roman Mars) turn the raw stuff of story into millions of downloads.

From the beginning of the book, the presumed universality of storytelling is evident. Addressing the similarities between podcasters and comic artists, Abel says, "We are all storytellers" (3), and a few pages later, Glass reiterates it: "I mean, it's story. We're makin' stories" (2015, 11). Collectively, the experts in this book offer a primer on how this particular type of storytelling is done, from conducting an effective interview, editing and re-editing until you've got it just right, to using sound design to build out the world of the story. Along the way, Abel paints a picture of the skill and nuance involved in this craft. What's striking about the book is that central paradox between the notion of story as self-evident, natural, and universal, and the emphasis on making stories as material, constraint-based, collaborative, and contested. The producers frequently disagree. Glass, for example, insists that "radio is a peculiarly didactic medium," and the producer's job is to tell the audience what the story means (qtd. in Abel 2015, 20), while Washington argues that the primary pleasure of listening is arriving at the moral yourself: "if I come to you and I tell you that story means this or a story means that, in that final little gap, I have robbed you of the ability to make the story your own" (qtd. in Abel 2015, 132). *Out on the Wire* shows us that story as a genre is highly produced—at one point, producers are experimenting with editing in "different breaths, to see which one sounds more natural" (2015, 32)—while insisting, again and again, that story is universal. Similarly, everyone can be a storyteller, but storytellers are experts.

If the creators of non-fiction radio and podcasts seem attached to the universality of story despite their own insistence on the craft involved in making it, it's because their notion of story is so firmly rooted in the sentimental mode, which is itself fascinated with the idea of universality and shared humanity. This investment is ideological and literal (as in financial); sentimental storytelling wouldn't be as popular or widespread if it weren't so good at smoothing the simultaneous flow of feeling and money (Klein 2003, 53). Christina Klein, in her work on the role of sentimentality in mid-twentieth-century American middlebrow culture, describes the sentimental as "a universalizing mode that imagines the possibility of transcending particularity by recognizing a common shared humanity" (Klein 2003, 14). While there's an emancipatory appeal in the idea of shared humanity, it's also double-edged: "in forging emotionally satisfying bonds across the divides of difference and in providing access to another's subjectivity, the sentimental could serve as an instrument for exercising power" (Klein 2003,

14–15). That power, in the history Klein is tracing, is the expansion of U.S. imperialism, rebranded as a kinder and gentler version of the British empire, perhaps most overtly embodied by the character of Anna in the musical *The King and I*. There's a clear line, in my mind at least, between Anna singing "Getting to Know You" to the children and wives of the King of Siam, and the master storytellers in *Out on the Wire* using personal stories to "help us to understand ourselves and our world a little bit better" (Abel 2015, back copy). Foundational to both is an approachable expert who is teaching us to see the rest of the world as fundamentally legible according to our own emotional vocabularies—and who is using that expertise and approachability to secure their own cultural power and financial gain.

A quick glance at news items emerging from the podcasting industry in the twenty-first century demonstrates how the approachable-expert personae of many white, male podcast hosts are entangled with their ability to both accumulate and misuse power. In December 2020, when the *New York Times* publicly retracted their podcast *Caliphate* for failing to meet their journalistic standards, the news led to a resurgence of conversations about the history of its producer Andy Mills. As writer Molly Osberg explains, Mills has been the subject of multiple "accusations of bullying and misogyny" from which, like the journalistic failures of *Caliphate*, he has emerged unscathed. This lack of consequences "invite[s] questions about who institutions like the *Times* are inclined to want to see succeed—and who might suffer as a result" (Osberg 2021). Only two months later, in February 2021, Gimlet Media's popular podcast *Reply All*'s investigative miniseries "The Test Kitchen" was cancelled mid-run amid revelations that the co-hosts, P.J. Vogt and Sruthi

Pinnamaneni, had created a toxic work environment at Gimlet akin to the one they were investigating at *Bon Appetit*'s "The Test Kitchen," actively opposing unionization attempts and harassing Black colleagues. As Erin Vanderhoof writes in *Vanity Fair*, these revelations were difficult for long-time fans of Gimlet's brand of podcasting:

> Part of the appeal of StartUp and Reply All came from their seeming commitment to honestly portraying its creators, warts and all. But these angry revelations from Gimlet staffers revealed the limits of that kind of public-facing honesty. With the help of a larger team, Vogt, [Reply All cohost Alex] Goldman, and [Gimlet co-founder and host of StartUp Alex] Blumberg all built characters that weren't necessarily reflective of what the environment in the company was like—but listeners were genuinely enamored by the fiction. (2021)

In the case of both *Caliphate* and "The Test Kitchen," the women of colour producers resigned, while men like Mills and Goldman faced few, if any, consequences. These "experts" have the power to decide whose stories are told and how, to define what constitutes the ordinary and the authentic, while hiding patterns of abuse under the persona of the sentimental storyteller, a persona deeply rooted in whiteness. If nothing else, these revelations remind us to be suspicious of the identities that have served as a screen for these patterns of harm, and in general of an industry that values authenticity over accountability.

In "Tell Me I'm Fat," Ira Glass has the role of the expert, curating and framing stories to make them comprehensible to his audience, helping us recognize the shared humanity of those we're getting to know. And, as in *The King and I*, there's power in deciding whose stories will be told and how they will be framed to evoke an emotional response in listeners. For those of us who are positioned as experts—whether we're standing at the front of a classroom or speaking into a microphone—the onus is on us to recognize the power that comes with these positions. And we need to think about how we can build accountability into our own practices, because powerful institutions are not going to do that for us. Part of that accountability process, for me, has been creating space for and honouring how my work impacts others, both intellectually and emotionally. Of the many things podcasting has taught me, perhaps the most vital is this: I never know who's listening. This is true in the classroom as well, where recognizing that I have no idea what's going on in the lives of my students, that I have no right to know, and that I must lean into this unknowability, has been vital to my own feminist pedagogy. Despite this recognition, though, relistening to "Tell Me I'm Fat" drove home something I hadn't fully realized before. Being the subject of sentimental storytelling is like being chosen for a team in a schoolyard game: sure, it feels good to be included, but there's always the stinging reminder that someone else got to decide whether you were included or not. When I have explored, in the past, the potential of sentimental storytelling to create social change by humanizing people, I've been in the position either of the reader, the one potentially learning from the stories, or the expert, teaching others how to read these stories. It is a very different feeling to be the one the story is humanizing. It's a reminder that people don't already think of you as human.

This is the reading I produce now, from the perspective of someone invested in politicized fat positivity that rejects the positioning of fatness as a personal and emotional problem. I now see how the episode uses Lindy West's personal "coming out" story as a fat person to frame fatness as an individual, even idiosyncratic choice, that some people (like West) can make while others (like Baker) may not. This framing of the episode via West and Glass's conversation undermines the structural critique offered in Baker's story and, differently, in Gay's interview, when she suggests that fatness as choice is complicated by race. The episode concludes with West telling the story of her husband's proposal, a response to her insistence that, as a fat woman, she also deserved to be seen as desirable and worthy. The politics of the episode get stuck at that revelation—a question of who can be seen, and how—without ever successfully moving the critique beyond individualization. But I can also see why the episode worked so well on me when I first listened to it. It felt powerful to hear stories that mirrored my own experiences; I felt drawn into shared emotional intimacy with the women I was listening to.

From this perspective, looking back at an education rife with sentimental stories, I have to pause and ask whether the sentimental framing of "Tell Me I'm Fat" via individual women's suffering is actually the problem. The episode worked for me then just as it was intended to, by creating an intimate public—and it did a particularly good job of that because podcasting is such an intimate medium. Even if the podcast itself doesn't do the work of pointing to systems of power and calling for social transformation, it did the thing that sentimentality does best: registering the deeply personal effects of social violence at the level of the mundane and the everyday. Does the fact that I look back on it with distress mean that it was never effective, or that it was a stepping stone for me, personally, to a different kind of politics? I learned to put my feelings back into my work in large part by taking up a medium that is invested in how stories make us feel. I am often suspicious of claims that compassion or empathy can move us beyond individual response, but my own shifting understanding of this very episode suggests something different: that sentimental responses can indeed be the starting point for political ones.

# COMING BACK TO CARE

**I COME BACK AGAIN AND AGAIN TO THE PROBLEM OF CARE.**
As a fat teenager at the very earliest stages of coming to terms with my body and my sexuality, my longing for care was entangled with the problem of desirability. I can't remember a time when I desired someone else, but I remember intensely the desire *to be* desired, and the awareness that my invisibility to men in particular was a problem—despite the fact that I was deeply uninterested in actually spending time with them. I was decades away from being able to articulate my longing to be with, admire, embrace, and celebrate women, non-binary, and gender non-conforming people as part of what feminist and queer studies scholar Ela Przybylo calls an asexual erotics, a term that encompasses "forms of intimacy that are simply not reducible to sex and sexuality and that, further, challenge the Freudian doxa that the sexual is at the base of all things" (2019, 20). Teenaged me

understood desire as romantic and heterosexual in its purest form. I've only recently learned about Gayle S. Rubin's concept of the "charmed circle," a visual representation of common hierarchies of different sex acts, with monogamous, heterosexual, reproductive sex between able-bodied cis white people at the centre (qtd. in Thom 2020). But back then, I was instinctively insulted when my best friend at the time suggested that, as a fat woman, I might have better luck dating other women. Lesbians, she told me, cared less about appearance.

This conversation was my first, but far from my last, experience of being explicitly rejected from the heterosexual order of desirability, a regime of racialized, gendered, and ableist power in which women are graded according to our value in the eyes of straight white men. It was also, confusingly, my first experience of being told that I might be gay. You will be astonished to hear that I did not spontaneously start dating women. Instead, I spent the next decade and a half struggling to understand my relationship to a body that seemed irreconcilable with any narratives of happiness or fulfillment I could find. As I got older, this frustrated sense of my own failure to do my gender correctly slowly led me away from the sentimental narratives of my childhood; hand in hand with an education that valued my capacity for critique above all else, I became convinced that care wasn't something I wanted or needed.

It's one thing to write theoretically about the search for narratives in which we can see ourselves, narratives that might function as models for other ways of being in the world—and quite another to really grapple with the ways our own legibility or illegibility as subjects worthy of care have material impacts on our lives.[1] In "Decrying Desirability, Demanding Care,"

Cree-Métis writer Samantha Marie Nock describes how the "economies of care" in late-stage capitalism dictate who we deem worthy of care, and that it tends to be reserved for romantic (particularly heterosexual and reproductive) relationships. "When you're on the other end of desirability politics," Nock writes, "and you live in a body that isn't deemed desirable by normative standards, you find your worlds in your friends" (2018). But the scarcity logics of capitalism constantly threaten the disappearance of those worlds, as people "deemed undesirable—among them, people who are fat, not white, queer, trans, disabled, or exist at any intersection of marginalization," grapple with the potential loss of our networks of care (Nock 2018). This loss can't be articulated as "merely" an emotional loss, though it is also that. But the whole tangled topic of desire and care wouldn't be so concerning if there wasn't also a material consideration. As Caleb Luna writes, care is about "commit[ting] to keeping each other alive despite our sexual capital" (2018).

The constant relocation built into academic life has sharpened my perspective on economies of care. When I first relocated from Edmonton to Vancouver to take up a tenure-track position, I struggled with how physically, painfully lonely I was. In all my years of training and professionalization, no one had warned me about the loneliness. Certainly, as a single and childless woman on the job market, I enjoyed a level of mobility that my partnered and/or parenting colleagues did not—in fact, not having a baby or being married made me more likely to get a tenure-track position. But what makes state-sanctioned relationships a detriment to women on the job market is the same thing that makes them a privilege: everyone, including the university, assumes they're coming with you. As a spinster—a term

I like to use for myself, and one I became comfortable with years before I started to identify as asexual—I'm about as productive as a woman can get because, from the perspective of the university, the rest of my life is a void, a question mark unoccupied by relationships and responsibilities.

In reality, however, my life is characterized not by the absence of relationships, but by the absence of the two relationships that the state and its institutions recognize. Relocating for a job thus means not also negotiating the relocation of other people (a difficulty I have no intention of underplaying), but rather coming face-to-face with the reality that, in writer and literature scholar Briallen Hopper's words, the "powerful forms of female love, friendship, commitment, and community" that structure my life don't—for better or for worse—count. The spinster, for Hopper, is defined not by lack but by a difference that threatens, and is in turn threatened by, the dominant reproductive norms. In her failure to define herself through marriage and childbearing, the spinster becomes invisible at best, and outright vilified at worst (Hopper 2015). As Przybylo puts it, "The spinster is a figure as much resonant with loneliness and the desexualization of aging as with inventing ways to survive in a couple-centric society that leaves single women with little space to flourish" (2019, 114). My professional relocation reminded me just how invisible my networks of care are in the eyes of the state. I've been reminded of this again by the COVID-19 pandemic, as communication around virus transmission consistently assumes normative, nuclear households, and fails to account for those of us who live alone, who cannot isolate in our homes while also satisfying our need for others.

The pandemic has also highlighted how access to care is unequally distributed along lines of class, race, age, and disability. Alongside the re-emergence of overt forms of white supremacist authoritarianism around the world, the systemic failures of the pandemic have signalled the death knell of the promises of sentimentality as a universalizing force that could bring us together across great divides. Instead, those divides have gotten wider. We feel them at multiple levels, as some of us stay home while others are forced out into the world to care for our needs, as Black, Indigenous, racialized, working class, disabled, and older people die at disproportionate rates while our governments do nothing to intervene, as anti-Asian racism surges, as vaccine distribution widens the gulf between a handful of wealthy developed nations and the rest of the world. And for those of us working within the university, we see how care is needed more urgently than ever, while continuing to be systemically undervalued.

There are ample studies indicating that women and racialized faculty—especially women of colour—take on significantly more emotional labour, particularly in relation to students. Articles on thriving in academia as a woman keep telling us to do less, to refuse the trap of caring too much. But this kind of refusal only contributes to the undervaluing of care work and feminized labour—and leaves our students more vulnerable to the institutions that constantly reframe their education, and their subjectivity, in brutally unfeeling terms. This is all the more evident in the midst of the pandemic: academics insisting on a business-as-usual adherence to notions of disinterested rigour look increasingly out of touch, as those of us who teach at universities and colleges are suddenly, unavoidably being reminded of our students' humanity and our own. In the university, as in the world, the pandemic has served as a reminder that institutions and systems will not save us. We are being collectively called upon to reimagine these systems in terms of an ethics of care.

But care—as deployed by corporations or the state— also will not save us. We need to be suspicious when institutions claim to care, and when care is being used to maintain, rather than dismantle, fundamentally dehumanizing systems. As Hiʻilei Julia Kawehipuaakahaopulani Hobart and Tamara Kneese explain, care can be co-opted by the state and other institutions "to extract unpaid labor" and "instrumentalize empathy and care to their own ends" (2020, 8). As the many inequities and injustices within the university and beyond are laid bare, care may be leveraged to patch over them and to help institutions maintain their imaginative force in the midst of this crisis, rather than being exposed as sites of neo-liberal profiteering. But what other options do we have? Teacher and scholar Brenna Clarke Gray summarizes this impasse in university-based care work:

A choice to resist calls for my emotional labour is also a choice to kick the ball down the road to someone else, someone who may not have the privileges of security and academic freedom that my faculty position—tenure-track only, to be sure, and thus precarious in its own way—affords me. Those of us who work in universities are hearing about the imminent budget crises that will befall the institution in the wake of Covid-19. Is there an ethical way to refuse to undertake this labour of care, of activism and agitation, from my position under these conditions? And if no one else continues the fight, if we do all revolt, is there a way for that to happen that doesn't leave students and truly precarious faculty as collateral damage, left to flounder without adequate supports? I cannot see one. (2020)

The refusal of care feels necessary, if we want to stop propping up extractive neo-liberal systems, and also impossible, if we refuse to abandon others to the violence of those systems. It is true that care can be co-opted, but it is also our only way forward. Christina Sharpe, in her critique of white supremacist and state-sanctioned forms of care, asks what it looks like to "think (and rethink and rethink) care laterally, in the register of the intramural, in a different relation than that of the violence of the state" (2016, 20). What forms of care might we envision that are not economized by the state, the university, or other institutions? How do we demand care while recognizing the harm that has been done in its name?

I want to imagine care as tending and as attending to. I want to imagine care as boundaried but limitless, beyond the scarcity logics of capitalism that tell us there isn't enough for everyone, that care for me must come at the cost of care for you. Sometimes care is enacted through refusal—staying home, turning down coercive or harmful medical interventions, refusing to subject your students to unethical surveillance technologies. Other times it takes the form of collective action, like the care webs created by "sick and disabled predominantly Black and brown queer people" that Leah Lakshmi Piepzna-Samarasinha describes in *Care Work: Dreaming Disability*

*Justice* (2018). As I recognize the limitations of the sentimental model of care, with its fantasies of a universal human experience, I can instead see how care is embedded in attention to the granular differences of people's everydays. This model of care, critical as it is of the capitalist and white supremacist logics of desirability, has much in common with Audre Lorde's work on erotics, which Przybylo describes as "a profound source of knowing otherwise" (2019, 23), resonating with Hobart and Kneese's conclusion that "radical care provides a roadmap for an otherwise" (2020, 142). Imagining otherwise "unlocks an attention to both the mundane and the revolutionary," reminding us that radical transformation so often begins at the most mundane levels (Przybylo 2019, 24).

As I seek to imagine a version of care that is not coercive or extractive, I keep returning to banal artistic forms invested in the detailing of minutia; the list, the anecdote, and the inventory all evoke Muñoz's queer ephemera, those traces that point to what is beyond representation (2009). In these forms, I find a space to practice care as loving attention and attending. They offer a moment of arrest, pause, in the fact of the everyday and its sheer banality, before that everyday can be expanded to signify something more universal. This unlocking of attention is at work in Dionne Brand's long poem *Inventory* (2006), an exploration of mediated witnessing in the wake of 9/11 that is at once invested in refusing the sentimental war-mongering of U.S. politics and committed to recognizing affective response as its own urgent political project.[2] *Inventory* enacts this commitment through the form of the inventory, a careful—and care-full—attention specifically to those who the state wants us to ignore. Operating in part within the sentimental tradition of narratives that centre women's emotional responses to geo-political events, *Inventory* also upends this tradition by asking who does the witnessing, and who is witnessed. The witness figure in the book is described as spending a year sitting

at the television weeping,
no reason,
the whole time (2006, 21)

That dismissal of the weeping being for "no reason" is a stark contrast to the reasons that follow, suggesting the way some forms of grief are more legitimized than others, and some lives more grievable.[3] The passage at once evokes the long history of women's politicized mourning, and insists that not all mourning is politicized equally.

As the title suggests, *Inventory* offers a series of lists—people, places, and events—that the speaker witnesses and mourns, tangling together an ethics of care with the risk of becoming numbed by the reality of so much human suffering. The rhythmic gesture of listing pushes back against that kind of emotional hardening—but *Inventory* also recognizes how attending to the suffering of others can be emptied of its political and ethical force when its end point is the witness's own emotional response, when, as Brand puts it, "we don't care beyond pity" (2006, 47). Toward the end of *Inventory*, the speaker explores the possibility of happiness, listing various sources of joy before turning aside their comfort as inimical to the project of witness:

I have nothing soothing to tell you,
that's not my job,

my job is to revise and revise this bristling list
hourly (Brand 2006, 100)

The endless and constant project of paying attention is both mundane and revolutionary; it also distinguishes between what is and is not the poet's responsibility. When we dwell, as I have in this book, on the question of how, and indeed whether, reading moves us to action, it's necessary to distinguish between the work of the text and the work of the reader. It's not my job, the speaker says, almost as though she is speaking for the poem itself. Texts are not themselves ethics, or a stand-in for action, nor can Black women be made to function as surrogate witnesses for sympathetic readers. Tending to these inventories of ignored things can be a starting point, but drawing the revolutionary potential out of the mundane detail—that is a different kind of work.

I've learned to look for inventories and ephemera as a reader, listener, and watcher; I've learned to pause and consider how those lists can teach me to see the world otherwise, in the banal specificity of a life's texture. I pause over Piepzna-Samarasinha's poem "I know crips live here" as she lists the evidence that marks a shared identity, from "A bathroom filled with coconut oil, unscented conditioner and black soap" to "the imprint of your ass in the couch surrounded by empty bags of food and the Advil and the heating pad" (*Tonguebreaker* 2019, 36). I pause over Bart Vautour's poem "Facts about Xanthippe" as he lists the distances of five asteroids named for maligned women—Xanthippe, Penelope, Beatrix, Godiva, and Yoko Ono—from Montreal on December 6, 1989, their "choreography of witness" to the École Polytechnique massacre; I see how poetry can make numbers into witnessing (2019). I pause over what Sara Ahmed puts in her "Killjoy Survival Kit," her books and things and tools and time and life and permission notes and other killjoys and humour and feelings and bodies (2017, 235–49); I consider what goes into my own kit, what traces I gather and inventory, anchoring myself to communities real and imagined.

I have been writing a list on my body, collaboratively, in tattoo ink. This list is a reclamation: it insists that my body is not a cage I'm struggling to free myself from, but the very substance of who and what I am. When it stops, I will also stop, like my mother did on a bleak November afternoon, fresh hair dye bleeding into her pillowcase, her last breaths witnessed by my brother and father, but not by me. I was out getting lunch.

The list I am writing on my body claims these pale limbs, with their stretch marks and cellulite; it claims these pendulous breasts, this round belly, these broad hips and thick thighs and wide feet. It began on my back: the outline of an echinacea flower, like the ones my mother grew in her garden, flowers she could see from the bedroom where she died, that she lovingly painted, harvested, and turned into medicine. The list grew down my left arm, as I populated it with more of her garden: with bleeding hearts and yarrow and wild blueberries and bee balm, with chickadees and garter snakes. These are the plants and creatures that she cared for, as she cared for me; carrying them on my body, they remind me that I am part of a lineage of women who care ferociously and imperfectly, women who are trying to make a world.

And now the list has grown down my right arm, an inventory of the tools I have found for myself as I have sought my own way through. Here is wheat, for the years I lived in Edmonton, Treaty 6 territory, and the face of the cat I adopted there; beneath, a stack of pancakes, for the cat I adopted in Vancouver. Here's a match, for my anger, and a semicolon, to remember the times in my life when I wanted to die, but didn't. Here are scissors and a knife, either tools or weapons, depending on how you hold them. And here, the parting words of *Secret Feminist Agenda*, the only words on this list. Scrawled across an envelope, surrounded by flowers, is a directive to myself and my beloveds, a reminder of the most practical thing we can do with our knowledge and our passions and our hard-gained insights, no matter how small.

Pass it on.

# ACKNOWLEDGEMENTS

I BEGAN WRITING THIS BOOK IN 2018, BUT IT HAS BEEN fermenting for much longer than that, as I have gradually re-imagined myself, my work, and my life.

In Edmonton, those transformations were made possible by a community that nurtured, inspired, witnessed, and affirmed me as I took shaky first steps into everything from podcasting to asexuality. My love and gratitude to all those people, who ensure that Edmonton will always feel like home. In November of 2021 I got to sit in a living room with Marcelle Kosman, Trevor Chow-Fraser, Clare Mulcahy, Todd Merkley, Kaitlin Trimble, Stephen Tchir, and their various babies and cats. We made music together, passing babies and refilling drinks and trying not to trip over cats or toys, and I was reminded that absolutely nothing has been more important to my development as a feminist and a critic than being so completed and unambiguously loved. My gratitude also to Andrea Hasenbank, Sylvie Vigneux, Rebecca Blakey, and Kristine Smitka, who have all pushed my thinking in different but equally transformative ways. You're all very good kitties.

In Vancouver, I've had the challenge and pleasure of building a new community almost entirely from scratch, and thus of filling my life with weirdos and artists and queers. The unexpected staying-put of the pandemic has made my roots here deeper and stronger than I ever imagined they would be. Love to Cynara Geissler, Don English, Andrea Warner, Aimee Ouellette, and Erika Thorkelson, the Fat Kids Book Club, a group of brilliant artists who I feel so privileged to think and learn alongside; to Zena Sharman, my femme Gemini mentor and idol; to Dina Del Bucchia, for teaching me to love the ocean; to Marshall Watson, for letting me describe this entire book in detail while we walked around Portland; to Nancy Fulton, Holly-Kate Collinson-Shield, Tara Newell, and Rachel Smith, for the music; to Ashra Kolhatkar, for teaching me to talk to cats; and to Hilary Atleo, for the books and the games and the hugs. I want to hang out with all of you, every day, forever.

Not all of my beloveds are nearby, but that doesn't mean they're any less beloved or any less integral to my thinking and growing. Love to my family, and to Cosette Derome, Jessie Ferne, and Vanessa Lakewood, my oldest friends, who knew me when my takes were really astonishingly bad, and yet somehow still love me; to Lucia Lorenzi and Brenna Clarke Gray, a.k.a. The Group Chat, a.k.a The Unicorn Crew, a.k.a Beef Friends, a.k.a Tuffy Feet, for showing me what feminist collaborative thinking can be; and to Erin Wunker, Bart Vautour, and E, for being my people.

This book might just have the one name on the cover, but its creation has been a deeply collaborative process. Thanks are due to the gorgeous feminist communities surrounding *Secret Feminist Agenda* and *Witch, Please*, from whom I have learned so much; to Erin Wunker and Emily Murphy, who read very early and unformed versions of this work; to Lucia Lorenzi, Aimee Ouellette, Zena Sharman, and Andrea Warner, my brilliant beta readers, for a thousand gentle pushes; and to my generous, thoughtful, and encouraging peer reviewers. Thanks to all my colleagues in the Publishing program at Simon Fraser University, for supporting my work no matter how troublemaking it was. And of course, none of this would have been possible without the incredible team at Wilfrid Laurier University Press, including Lisa Quinn, Murray Tong, Clare Hitchens, Maia Desjardins, Lindsey Hunnewell, and Siobhan McMenemy, who has been patiently helping me find my voice for years now.

Finally, and forever, thanks to my mother, Teresa Joan Penner. I miss you.

# NOTES

### Territory Acknowledgement

1   I learned about these territories both from living on them and from consulting the websites of each nation, which at the time of writing are https://www.musqueam.bc.ca/, https://www.squamish.net/, and https://twnation.ca/.

2   I use "we" when discussing whiteness to grammatically avoid distancing myself from the violence entangled in this racial identity, fully recognizing that you, the reader, may not be part of this "we."

3   Reckoning with the ongoing legacy of residential schools is vital work for settlers living in what is currently called Canada. Starting in May of 2021, when 200 unmarked graves were discovered on Tk'emlúps te Secwépemc territory at the site of the Kamloops Indian Residential School, dozens of new investigations have begun, seeking proof of what residential school

survivors have been saying all along: that these places were "schools" in name only, and were in fact detention camps for children with astonishingly high death rates alongside institutionally sanctioned patterns of neglect and abuse. For more information, consult the reports of the National Truth and Reconciliation Commission.

### A Sentimental Education

1   That's Belle, by the way, in the Disney film *Beauty and the Beast*, chafing against the assumption that she will marry and settle into a live of domestic servitude. Never mind that the happy ending is, in fact, her marriage.

2   This concept of reading the right things in the right ways comes from Richard Altick's *The English Common Reader*, a study of the emergence of widespread literacy in nineteenth-century England and the accompanying anxiety that the "common" reader would somehow do it wrong: "it was not enough to cultivate the desire to read good books; just as important was the necessity for showing the masses of people *how* to read" (1998, 372).

3   As recently as 2011 *The New Yorker* published an article doing just this called "'Uncle Tom's Cabin' and the Art of Persuasion" (Gordon-Reed).

4   For more on the use of racial violence as a technology of white self-improvement, see Saidya V. Hartman's *Scenes of Subjection: Terror, Slavery, and Self-Making in Nineteenth-Century America* (1997).

5   For more on the role of literature in the development of racial liberalism, see Jodi Melamed's *Represent and Destroy: Rationalizing Violence in the New Racial Capitalism* (2011).

6   I am inspired, in this approach, by Janice Radway's *A Feeling for Books: The Book-of-the-Month Club, Literary Taste, and Middle-Class Desire* (1997), which marries book history and personal reading history to better understand the mediating roles of cultural institutions and how these interact with our individual experiences of reading.

7   The bunny, like Kobabe, uses Spivak pronouns, e/em/eir.

8   See, for example, Shannon Keating's "The New 'Little Women' Makes Space for Jo's Queerness" in *BuzzFeed News*.

## Caring Ferociously

1   In *Dear Science and Other Stories*, McKittrick returns multiple times to the question of "how I know what I know, where I know from, who I know from, and what I cannot possibly know" (2021, 14), and expresses deep suspicion of "the ways in which many academic methodologies refuse black life and relational thinking" (120).

2   Lorde's writing, here, recalls Michel Foucault's definition of bio-politics as articulated in "Society Must Be Defended," his Collège de France seminar from 1975–76. The function of biopower, he explains, is "to make live and to let die." I hesitate to attribute this line of thinking to Foucault, however, largely because the tradition of rooting concepts in the work of a handful of white men elides the long histories of intellectual work done by women and people of colour. I'm reminded of Simone Brown's argument that surveillance studies have been overly dependent on Foucault's concept of the panopticon, ignoring the fact that Jeremy Bentham (inventor of the panopticon) based the model in part on the holds of slave ships (see Brown's *Dark Matters: On the Surveillance of Blackness*, 2015).

3    As I write this, we are in the midst of a political movement led
     by Black Lives Matter that is fighting for police defunding and
     abolition during a global pandemic that is disproportionately
     killing Black people. These protests were spurred by the mur-
     der in 2020 of George Floyd at the hands of a police officer in
     Minneapolis, Minnesota as three other officers watched, and the
     murder of Breonna Taylor in her own home by police officers the
     same year. A new wave of conversations about white people's
     need to address our own participation in white supremacy and
     anti-Black violence—in order to commit to meaningful, systemic
     change—is unfolding across social media, in institutions, and
     within our intimate relationships.

### #Relatable

1    See Lauren Fournier's *Autotheory as Feminist Practice in Art,
     Writing, and Criticism* (2021) for an expansive discussion of
     autotheory's many forms.
2    My understanding of how authenticity is monetized within
     influencer culture is strongly informed by the pop culture com-
     mentary podcast *Who? Weekly*, a discussion of contemporary
     celebrity and its mediation (Finger and Weber, 2012–present).
3    They spoke as part of The Bonham Centre for Sexual Diversity
     Studies at the University of Toronto's Lynch Distinguished
     Lecturer Series. The event took place over Zoom on November
     19, 2020.

### Words with Friends

1    When I quoted this line in *Witch, Please,* Book 4 Episode 4, "Post-
     Critique," Marcelle pointed out that the reference to not being
     able to eat just one is, in fact, the slogan of Lays potato chips,

thus demonstrating one of the greatest scholarly pleasures: nit-picking.

2   In February of 2018, with the financial support of *Witch, Please* listeners, Marcelle and I visited The Wizarding World of Harry Potter at Universal Orlando. It was a remarkable and joyful experience, and the recognition that I am no longer comfortable giving money to J.K. Rowling in this way is a little heartbreaking; sometimes letting go of your objects hurts, even when you know they are a barrier to your and your community's thriving.

3   This critical stance is entwined with New Criticism, Roland Barthes's notion of the death of the author, and the canonization of literary modernism, all shifts in the academic study of literature that enshrined the critic as the locus of textual meaning rather than the author (1977).

4   This line comes from an apology Marcelle wrote for the beginning of *Witch, Please,* 2.8; I played a recording of this apology in a *Secret Feminist Agenda* live bonus episode, "Podcasting, Public Scholarship, and Accountability" (posted November 23, 2017).

### Getting to Know You

1   See episode 4.12, "Cool Poet Mom with Dina Del Bucchia."

### Coming Back to Care

1   In *Ace: What Asexuality Reveals about Desire, Society, and the Meaning of Sex*, Angela Chen outlines many of the ways that romantic love is legally valued over other relationships, "including over 1,100 laws that benefit married couples at the federal level" (2020, 131).

2   In *Poetry Matters: Neoliberalism, Affect, and the Posthuman in Twenty-First Century North American Feminist Poetics*, Heather

Milne links Brand's work to the "Public Feelings Project," created by Ann Cvetkovich, Lauren Berlant, Kathleen Stewart, and other feminist scholars to assert "the value of bringing 'emotional sensibilities to bear on intellectual projects'" (Milne 2018, 157).

3 For more on grievability as a register of the unequal distribution of humanity, see Judith Butler's *Precarious Life: The Powers of Mourning and Violence* (2006).

# WORKS CITED

Abel, Jessica. *Out on the Wire: The Storytelling Secrets of the New Masters of Radio*. New York: Broadway Books, 2015.

Ahmed, Sara. *Living a Feminist Life*. Durham, NC: Duke University Press, 2017.

———. "Selfcare as Warfare." *Feministkilljoys* (blog). August 25, 2014. https://feministkilljoys.com/2014/08/25/selfcare-as-warfare/.

Alcott, Louisa May. *Little Women*. Boston, MA: Roberts Brothers, 1869.

———. *An Old-Fashioned Girl*. Boston, MA: Roberts Brothers, 1870.

Altick, Richard D. *The English Common Reader: A Social History of the Mass Reading Public, 1800–1900*. Columbus, OH: Ohio State University Press, 1998.

Aluli-Meyer, Manulani. "Changing the Culture of Research: An Introduction to the Triangulation of Meaning." *Hūlili:*

*Multidisciplinary Research on Hawaiian Well-Being* 3, no. 1 (2006): 263–79.

Arjini, Nawal. "The Trouble with White Women: An Interview with Kyla Schuller." *The Nation*, November 26, 2018. https://www .thenation.com/article/the-trouble-with-white-women-an -interview-with-kyla-schuller/.

Ascher, Carol, Louise DeSalvo, and Sarah Ruddick, eds. *Between Women: Biographers, Novelists, Critics, Teachers and Artists Write about Their Work on Women*. Boston, MA: Beacon Press, 1984.

Atwood, Margaret. *Surfacing*. Toronto, ON: McClelland & Stewart, 1972.

Austen, Jane. *Pride and Prejudice*. London: T. Egerton, 1813.

Baldwin, James. *Notes of a Native Son*. Boston, MA: Beacon Press, 1984.

Barthes, Roland. *Image-Music-Text*. Trans. Stephen Heath. New York: Hill and Wang, 1977.

Belcourt, Billy-Ray. "Settler Structures of Bad Feeling." *Canadian Art*, January 8, 2018. https://canadianart.ca/essays/ settler-structures-bad-feeling/.

Bennett, Laura. "The First-Person Industrial Complex." *Slate*, September 14, 2015. http://www.slate.com/articles/life/ technology/2015/09/the_first_person_industrial_complex_how_ the_harrowing_personal_essay_took.html.

Berlant, Lauren. *The Female Complaint: The Unfinished Business of Sentimentality in American Culture*. Durham, NC: Duke University Press, 2008.

———. "The Unfinished Business of Cruel Optimism." Paper presented at The Bonham Centre for Sexual Diversity Studies in the University of Toronto's Lynch Distinguished Lecturer Series, Toronto, ON, November 19, 2020.

Bob-Waksberg, Raphael, creator. *BoJack Horseman*. Season 1, episode 5, "Live Fast, Diane Nguyen." Netflix, 2014.

Bowen, Leah-Simone, and Falen Johnson. *The Secret Life of Canada*. "Shout Out to Susan Olivia Poole." Podcast mini-episode, October 17, 2017. https://thesecretlifeofcanada.libsyn.com/website/shout-out-to-susan-olivia-poole.

Bowering, George. *Kerrisdale Elegies*. Vancouver, BC: Talonbooks, 1984, reprinted 2008.

Brand, Dionne. *Inventory*. Toronto, ON: McClelland & Stewart, 2006.

Brown, Simone. *Dark Matters: On the Surveillance of Blackness*. Durham, NC: Duke University Press, 2015.

Butler, Judith. *Gender Trouble: Feminism and the Subversion of Identity*. London: Routledge, 2006.

———. *Precarious Life: The Powers of Mourning and Violence*. New York: Verso Books, 2004.

Butler, Octavia E. *Kindred*. Garden City, NY: Doubleday, 1979.

Cahalan, Susannah. "'Goodnight Moon' Author Was a Bisexual Rebel Who Didn't like Kids." *New York Post*, January 7, 2017. https://nypost.com/2017/01/07/goodnight-moon-author-was-a-bisexual-rebel-who-hated-kids/.

Campbell, Donna M. "Sentimental Conventions and Self-Protection: *Little Women* and *The Wide, Wide World*." *Legacy* 11, no. 2 (1994): 118–29.

de Certeau, Michel. *The Practice of Everyday Life*. Translated by Steven F. Rendall, vol. 1. Los Angeles, CA: University of California Press, 1998.

Chen, Angela. *Ace: What Asexuality Reveals about Desire, Society, and the Meaning of Sex*. Boston, MA: Beacon Press, 2020.

Clare, Eli. *Brilliant Imperfection: Grappling with Cure*. Durham, NC: Duke University Press, 2017.

Couldry, Nick. "Digital Storytelling, Media Research and Democracy: Conceptual Choices and Alternative Futures." *Digital Storytelling, Mediatized Stories: Self-Representations in New Media*, edited by Knut Lundby, 41–60. New York: Peter Lang, 2008.

Darnton, Robert. *The Great Cat Massacre and Other Episodes in French Cultural History*. New York: Basic Books, 1984.

Driscoll, Beth. *The New Literary Middlebrow*. London: Palgrave Macmillan UK, 2014.

@dumb_dyke_tears. "for a lot of white queers (esp those who are mentally ill) the entire concept of 'self-care' becomes a stagnation point where we never move beyond seeking our own comfort. but when white people prioritize our own comfort over all else, it inevitably leads to white supremacy." *Twitter*, June 13, 2020. Tweet deleted.

Echlin, Kim. *The Disappeared*. Toronto, ON: Penguin Canada, 2010.

Eliot, T.S. *The Waste Land*. New York: Boni & Liveright, 1922.

Eve, Martin Paul. *Open Access and the Humanities: Contexts, Controversies and the Future*. Cambridge: Cambridge University Press, 2014. https://doi.org/10.1017/CBO9781316161012.

Finger, Bobby, and Lindsey Weber. *Who? Weekly*. Podcast, 2016–present. https://www.whoweekly.us/.

Fink, Joseph, and Jeffrey Cranor. *Welcome to Night Vale*. Podcast, 2012–present. https://www.welcometonightvale.com/.

Fitzgerald, F. Scott. *The Great Gatsby*. New York: Charles Scribner's Sons, 1925.

Foucault, Michel. *Discipline and Punish: The Birth of the Prison*. New York: Pantheon Books, 1977.

———. *"Society Must Be Defended": Lectures at the Collège de France, 1975–1976*. Translated by David Macey. London: Picador, 2003.

Fournier, Lauren. *Autotheory as Feminist Practice in Art, Writing, and Criticism*. Cambridge, MA: MIT Press, 2021.

Fung, Amy. *Before I Was a Critic I Was a Human Being*. Toronto, ON: Book*hug Press, 2019.

Georgakopoulou, Alexandra. "From Narrating the Self to Posting Self(ies): A Small Stories Approach to Selfies." *Open Linguistics* 2, no. 1 (Jan. 2016). doi:10.1515/opli-2016-0014.

Gerwig, Greta, dir. *Little Women*. 2019; Culver City, CA: Sony Pictures.

Gibb, Camilla. *Sweetness in the Belly*. Toronto, ON: Anchor Canada, 2006.

Glass, Ira. *This American Life*. "Tell Me I'm Fat." Podcast, 589, June 17, 2016. https://www.thisamericanlife.org/589/tell-me-im-fat.

Gordon-Reed, Annette. "The Art of Persuasion: Harriet Beecher Stowe's 'Uncle Tom's Cabin.'" *The New Yorker*, June 6, 2011. https://www.newyorker.com/magazine/2011/06/13/the-persuader-annette-gordon-reed.

Gorman, Sarah. "'You Can Say Much More Interesting Things about a Scar, than You Can About a Wound' – Selina Thompson's Salt. as an Act of Radical Softness.'" *Readingasawoman* (blog). August 16, 2019. https://readingasawoman.wordpress.com/2019/08/16/you-can-say-much-more-interesting-things-about-a-scar-than-you-can-about-a-wound-selina-thompsons-salt-as-an-act-of-radical-softness/.

Gray, Brenna Clarke. "Guest Post: Pedagogy of the So Stressed: Pivoting to Digital with an Ethics of Care." *Hook & Eye* (blog). April 27, 2020. https://hookandeye.ca/category/compassion/.

Green, Jesse. "The Gay History of America's Classic Children's Books." *The New York Times*, February 7, 2019. https://www.nytimes.com/2019/02/07/t-magazine/gay-children-book-authors.html

Gregg, Melissa. "A Mundane Voice." *Cultural Studies* 18, no. 203 (June 2010): 363–83.

Halpern, Faye. "Unmasking Criticism: The Problem with Being a Good Reader of Sentimental Rhetoric." *Narrative* 19, no. 1 (2011): 51–71. doi:10.1353/nar.2011.0005.

Hartman, Saidya V. *Scenes of Subjection: Terror, Slavery, and Self-Making in Nineteenth-Century America*. New York: Oxford University Press, 1997.

Hersey, Trisha. *The Nap Ministry* (blog). https://thenapministry. wordpress.com/.

Hobart, Hiʻilei Julia Kawehipuaakahaopulani, and Tamara Kneese. "Radical Care: Survival Strategies for Uncertain Times." *Social Text* 38, no. 1 (2020): 1–16.

Hochman, Barbara. "Uncle Tom's Cabin in the National Era: An Essay in Generic Norms and the Contexts of Reading." *Book History* 7 (2004): 143–69.

Hopper, Briallen. "On Spinsters." *Los Angeles Review of Books*, July 12, 2015. https://lareviewofbooks.org/article/on-spinsters/.

Howard, June. "What Is Sentimentality?" *American Literary History* 11, no. 1 (1999): 63–81.

Isay, Dave. "Everyone Around You Has a Story the World Needs to Hear." *Reality Radio: Telling True Stories in Sound*, edited by John Biewen and Alexa Dilworth. Second Ed., Revised and Expanded. Greenville, NC: University of North Carolina Press, 2017.

Jackson, Lauren Michele. "What Is an Anti-Racist Reading List For?" *Vulture*, June 2020. https://www.vulture.com/2020/06/anti -racist-reading-lists-what-are-they-for.html.

Jamison, Leslie. *The Empathy Exams: Essays*. Minneapolis, MN: Graywolf Press, 2014.

Johns, Jessica. *How Not to Spill*. Vancouver, BC: Rahila's Ghost Press, 2018.

Keating, Shannon. "The New 'Little Women' Makes Space for Jo's Queerness." *BuzzFeed News*, January 2, 2020. https://www.buzzfeednews.com/article/shannonkeating/little-women-greta-gerwig-saoirse-ronan-jo-march-queer.

Kiesewetter, Rebekka. "Undoing Scholarship: Towards an Activist Genealogy of the OA Movement." *Tijdschrift Voor Genderstudies* 23, no. 2 (2020): 113–30. doi:10.5117/TVGN2020.2.001.KIES.

Klein, Christina. *Cold War Orientalism: Asia in the Middlebrow Imagination, 1945–1961*. Los Angeles, CA: University of California Press, 2003.

Kobabe, Maia. "The Nonbinary Bunny." *Red Gold Sparks Press*, 2019. https://redgoldsparkspress.com/projects/7121743.

Kosman, Marcelle, and Hannah McGregor. *Witch, Please*. Podcast, 2015–present. https://play.acast.com/s/oh-witch-please.

Kretzmer, Herbert. "I Dreamed a Dream." Lyrics from *Les Misérables*, music by Alain Boublil and Claude Michel-Schönenberg (Original Broadway Cast Recording). Verve, 1987.

Lai, Larissa. *The Tiger Flu*. Vancouver, BC: Arsenal Pulp Press, 2018.

Lavery, Daniel M. *Something That May Shock and Discredit You*. New York: Simon & Schuster, 2020.

Lee, Dennis. *Alligator Pie*. Toronto, ON: Macmillan, 1974.

———. *Civil Elegies and Other Poems*. Toronto, ON: Anansi, 1972.

———. *Lizzy's Lion*. Illustrated by Marie-Louise Gay. Markham, ON: Fitzhenry & Whiteside, 1984.

Leslie, Alex. *We All Need to Eat*. Toronto, ON: Book*hug Press, 2018.

Lighthall, William Douw, editor. *Songs of the Great Dominion: Voices from the Forests and Waters, the Settlements and Cities of Canada*. Edinburgh: Walter Scott, 1889.

Liu, Rebecca. "The Making of a Millennial Woman." *Another Gaze: A Feminist Film Journal*, June 12, 2019. http://www.anothergaze .com/making-millennial-woman-feminist-capitalist-fleabag -girls-sally-rooney-lena-dunham-unlikeable-female-character -relatable/.

Lorde, Audre. *A Burst of Light: Essays*. Ann Arbor, MI: Firebrand Books, 1988.

Lorenzi, Lucia (@empathywarrior). "Still Tender." *Instagram*, May 9, 2018. https://www.instagram.com/p/BiksSVZldXF/.

Luna, Caleb. "Romantic Love Is Killing Us: Who Takes Care of Us When We Are Single?" *The Body Is Not an Apology*, September 18, 2018. https://thebodyisnotanapology.com/magazine/ romantic-love-is-killing-us/.

Machado, Carmen Maria. *In the Dream House*. Minneapolis, MN: Graywolf Press, 2019.

Malik, Rachel. "Horizons of the Publishable: Publishing in/as Literary Studies." *ELH* 75, no. 3 (2008): 707–35. doi:10.1353/ elh.0.0016.

Marlatt, Daphne. *Steveston*. Vancouver, BC: Talonbooks, 1974.

McDougall, Robert L. "Duncan Campbell Scott." *The Canadian Encyclopedia*, Historica Canada, August 11, 2008. https://www .thecanadianencyclopedia.ca/en/article/duncan-campbell-scott.

McGrath, Laura. "Comping White." *Los Angeles Review of Books*, January 21, 2019. https://lareviewofbooks.org/article/ comping-white/.

McGregor, Hannah. "'I Needed to See the Politic Being Lived': Virgie Tovar on Fat Activism and Digital Platforms." *Atlantis: Critical Studies in Gender, Culture & Social Justice* 38, no. 2 (Dec. 2017): 144–51.

————. *Secret Feminist Agenda*. Podcast (seasons 1–4). 2017–2020. https://secretfeministagenda.com/.

McKittrick, Katherine. *Dear Science and Other Stories*. Durham, NC: Duke University Press, 2021.

McLean, Susan. "'Radical Softness As A Weapon' Lora Mathis Writes What We're Too Afraid to Feel." *BRUISED KNUCKLES*, August 8, 2015. http://bruisedknuckles.weebly.com/17/post/2015/10/radical-softness-as-a-weapon-lora-mathis-writes-what-were-too-afraid-to-feel-by-susan-mclean.html.

McWilliam, Kelly, and Sharon Bickle. "Digital Storytelling and the 'Problem' of Sentimentality." *Media International Australia* 165, no. 1 (Nov. 2017): 77–89. doi:10.1177/1329878X17726626.

Mead, Rebecca. "The Scourge of 'Relatability.'" *The New Yorker*, August 12, 2014. https://www.newyorker.com/culture/cultural-comment/scourge-relatability.

Melamed, Jodi. *Represent and Destroy: Rationalizing Violence in the New Racial Capitalism*. Minneapolis, MN: University of Minnesota Press, 2011.

Mesle, Sarah. "Dickinson's Hair." *Los Angeles Review of Books*, January 21, 2021. https://lareviewofbooks.org/article/dickinsons-hair/.

Milne, Heather. *Poetry Matters: Neoliberalism, Affect, and the Posthuman in Twenty-First Century North American Feminist Poetics*. Iowa City, IA: University of Iowa Press, 2018.

Moi, Toril. *Revolution of the Ordinary: Literary Studies After Wittgenstein, Austin, and Cavell*. Chicago, IL: University of Chicago Press, 2017.

Moten, Fred, and Stefano Harney. "The University and the Undercommons: Seven Theses." *Social Text* 22, no. 2 (May 2004): 101–15.

Muñoz, José Esteban. *Cruising Utopia: The Then and There of Queer Futurity*. New York: NYU Press, 2009.

Narula, Svati Kirsten. "What's Wrong with Sentimentality?" *The Atlantic*, April 9, 2014. https://www.theatlantic.com /entertainment/archive/2014/04/whats-wrong-with -sentimentality/360355/.

National Centre for Truth and Reconciliation. "Reports." 2021. https://nctr.ca/records/reports/.

Nock, Samantha Marie. "Decrying Desirability, Demanding Care." *GUTS Magazine*, January 24, 2018. http://gutsmagazine.ca/ decrying-desirability-demanding-care/.

Osberg, Molly. "Inside the Caliphate Debacle, and Exactly Who Is Allowed to Fail." *Jezebel*, January 25, 2021. https://jezebel .com/inside-the-caliphate-debacle-and-exactly-who-is -allowe-1846041501.

Piepzna-Samarasinha, Leah Lakshmi. *Care Work: Dreaming Disability Justice*. Vancouver, BC: Arsenal Pulp Press, 2018.

———. *Tonguebreaker: Poems and Performance Texts*. Vancouver, BC: Arsenal Pulp Press, 2019.

Poletti, Anna. "Coaxing an Intimate Public: Life Narrative in Digital Storytelling." *Continuum* 25, no. 1 (Feb. 2011): 73–83. doi:10.1080/ 10304312.2010.506672.

———. "Review by Anna Poletti." *Wilfrid Laurier University Press*. https://www.wlupress.wlu.ca/Scholarly-Podcasting-Open-Peer -Review/Secret-Feminist-Agenda/Season-2/Scholarly-Reviews -of-the-Secret-Feminist-Agenda-Podcast-s2/Review-by-Anna -Poletti. Accessed February 11, 2021.

Przybylo, Ela. *Asexual Erotics: Intimate Readings of Compulsory Sexuality*. Columbus, OH: Ohio State University Press, 2019. https://ohiostatepress.org/books/titles/9780814214046.html.

Radway, Janice. *A Feeling for Books: The Book-of-the-Month Club, Literary Taste, and Middle-Class Desire*. Greenville, NC: University of North Carolina Press, 1997.

Richardson, Samuel. *Pamela; or, Virtue Rewarded*. London: Messrs Rivington & Osborn, 1740.

Robinson, Eden. *Trickster Drift*. Toronto, ON: Penguin Random House Canada, 2018.

Rothblum, Esther, and Sondra Solovay, eds. *The Fat Studies Reader*. New York: NYU Press, 2009. https://nyupress.org/9780814776315/the-fat-studies-reader.

Roupenian, Kristen. "Cat Person." *The New Yorker*, December 11, 2017. https://www.newyorker.com/magazine/2017/12/11/cat-person.

Rousseau, Jean-Jacques. *Julie; or, The New Heloise*. United Provinces: Marc-Michel Ray, 1761.

Roy, Wendy. *The Next Instalment: Serials, Sequels, and Adaptations of Nellie L. McClung, L.M. Montgomery, and Mazo de La Roche*. Waterloo, ON: Wilfrid Laurier University Press, 2019.

Ruddick, Lisa. "When Nothing Is Cool." *The Point Magazine*, December 7, 2015. https://thepointmag.com/2015/criticism/when-nothing-is-cool.

Schuller, Kyla. *The Biopolitics of Feeling: Race, Sex, and Science in the Nineteenth Century*. Durham, NC: Duke University Press, 2018.

Schwartz, Andi. "The Cultural Politics of Softness." *GUTS Magazine*, December 13, 2018. http://gutsmagazine.ca/the-cultural-politics-of-softness/.

Sharpe, Christina. *In the Wake: On Blackness and Being*. Durham, NC: Duke University Press, 2016.

Shraya, Vivek. *even this page is white*. Vancouver, BC: Arsenal Pulp Press, 2016.

Simon, Sarah. "The Feminist History of Fat Liberation." *Ms. Magazine*, October 18, 2019. https://msmagazine.com/2019/10/18/the-feminist-history-of-fat-liberation/.

Sims, Jonathan. *The Magnus Archives*. Podcast. Directed and produced by Alexander J. Newall. 2016–present. https://rustyquill.com/the-magnus-archives/.

Smith, Sidonie, and Julia Watson. "Virtually Me: A Toolbox about Online Self-Presentation." In *Identity Technologies: Constructing the Self Online*, ed. Anna Poletti and Julie Rak, 70–96. Madison, WI: University of Wisconsin Press, 2014.

Smyth, Melissa. "On Sentimentality: A Critique of Humans of New York." *Warscapes*, January 16, 2015. http://warscapes.com/opinion/sentimentality-critique-humans-new-york.

Sorfleet, John R. "Dennis Lee." *The Canadian Encyclopedia*, Historica Canada, February 10, 2008. https://thecanadianencyclopedia.ca/en/article/dennis-lee.

Sow, Aminatou, and Ann Friedman. *Big Friendship: How We Keep Each Other Close*. New York: Simon & Schuster, 2020.

Stowe, Harriet Beecher. *Uncle Tom's Cabin; or, Life Among the Lowly*. Boston: John P. Jewett and Company, 1852.

Strings, Sabrina. *Fearing the Black Body: The Racial Origins of Fat Phobia*. New York: NYU Press, 2019.

TallBear, Kim. "Failed Settler Kinship, Truth and Reconciliation, and Science." *Indigenous STS*, March 16, 2016. https://indigenoussts.com/failed-settler-kinship-truth-and-reconciliation-and-science/.

Thieme, Katja. "Do We Need New Method Names? Descriptions of Method in Scholarship on Canadian Literature." *ESC: English Studies in Canada* 44, no. 1 (2017): 91–110. doi:10.1353/esc.2017.0049.

Thom, Kai Cheng. "I'm an Old, Out and Proud Lesbian. Am I Transphobic If I Don't Want to Have Sex with Trans Women?" *Xtra Magazine*, September 15, 2020. https://xtramagazine.com/love-sex/lesbian-trans-women-attraction-179626.

Tolentino, Jia. *Trick Mirror: Reflections on Self-Delusion*. Toronto, ON: Penguin Random House, 2019.

Tuck, Eve, and K. Wayne Yang. "Decolonization Is Not a Metaphor." *Decolonization: Indigeneity, Education & Society* 1, no. 1, (2012): 1–40.

Vanderhoof, Erin. "Reply All's Implosion Reveals the Limits of One-Sided Internet Relationships." *Vanity Fair*, February 26, 2021. https://www.vanityfair.com/style/2021/02/reply-all-podcast-pause-resignations.

Vautour, Bart. *The Truth About Facts*. Picton, ON: Invisible Publishing, 2019.

Wagner, Kate. "Don't Let People Enjoy Things." *The Baffler*, May 9, 2019. https://thebaffler.com/kate-takes/dont-let-people-enjoy-things-wagner.

West, Lindy. *Shrill: Notes from a Loud Woman*. New York: Hachette, 2016.

Whitehead, Colson. *The Underground Railroad*. Garden City, NY: Doubleday, 2016.

Wise Brown, Margaret. *The Runaway Bunny*. Illustrated by Clement Hurd. New York: Harper, 1942.

Wunker, Erin. *Notes from a Feminist Killjoy: Essays on Everyday Life*. Toronto, ON: Book*hug Press, 2016.

Yao, Xine. *Disaffected: The Cultural Politics of Feeling in Nineteenth-Century America*. Durham, NC: Duke University Press, 2021.

# INDEX